In style of Paul Gilbert

by Toni Lloret

www.tonilloret.net

ISBN-13 978-1482790818 / ISBN-10 1482790815

Audio and video samples in:
www.tonilloret.net/paulgilbert/

Table of contents

Introduction:

Paul Gilbert is a guitarist who amazed me since the first time I heard of him, and from that moment it's been a high influence to me and a model to follow, specially his flawless right-hand's picking technique. Honestly I think Gilbert brought so much to guitar's world, and with no doubt he's one guitarist of those who deserves to study his style.

I've tried to capture in this book everything I've learned from him in a clear and tidy manner, so it could be easyly accessible for any student no matter what his level is. Gilbert has many virtues, but this book focuses on his technique. We'll see his favourite sequences, scales, patterns, string skipping, arpeggios, etc. All of it in a organized way with progressive difficulty exercises, it doesn't mean (for instance) we can't pass from exercise 1 to 2 before exercise 1 it's perfect, always we should go forward and come back and try again that exercise which we could not make it sound well at all, is another way to see our progress.

No tempo is indicated in exercises, the most important thing is what we play it's well played and sounds good. In any case it's suggested to use the metronome with the practice and see our speed progress, always minding it sounds good and it sounds every single note. As an orientation I estimate the fast runs of **Paul Gilbert** are commonly 16ths up to 220 BPM, 16ths sextuplets up to 140 BPM and 32ths up to 110 BPM. Maybe there are faster guitarists, but no one sounds like Gilbert.

I hope you enjoy this little tribute to **Paul Gilbert**, and specially I hope it will help you to improve your technique.

Thanks to:

Paul Gilbert and all the great guitarists who inspired and influenced me to write this book.

Ibanezgirl2 from deviantart.com for let me use her drawing in the front page.

Thanks too for their drawings to Strutsi (page 25), Rocío Ceballos (page 62), wimpified (pag 65).

My students and my teachers friends from the academy **www.GuitarraModerna.com**

And of course thanks to **you,** by purchasing this book, I honestly desire it will help you to improve.

Inquiries and contact: ***www.tonilloret.net***

Basic exercises

In this first section of the book we'll see some exercises, it could be said these are the basics of **Paul Gilbert**'s technique, so it's important to pay maximum attention and practice them as much as possible to improve the coordination between both hands and the "alternate picking" technique, one of the most difficult techniques to master in electric guitar.

Practice these exercises with patience, the better you nail these exercises the better will sound the rest of the examples of the book. Use a metronome, a rhythm box (or a drum base) to practice the exercises, also it's good to practice them sometimes without a metronome too.

Be careful with the suggested pick strokes in every exercise. The suggested strokes are shown by the symbols ⊓ (downstroke) and ∨ (upstroke). **It's important you really take care to the strokes and play them as suggested in every exercise** (downstroke when is shown a downstroke, upstroke when is shown an upstroke).

Left-hand fingering is indicated in the score too, the numbers that appears at the left of the notes in the score. Each number represents a left-hand finger, so number 1 represents the index finger, number 2 the middle finger, number 3 the ring finger, and number 4 the pinky finger. Left-hand fingering is the suggested fingering or "standard fingering", but if you feel comfortable using other kind of fingering feel free to use it, possibly the fingering suggested or "standard fingering" could be the most comfortable fingering for you too.

In these exercises, as well as in the rest of the book, **we should priorize always quality over speed. Paul Gilbert** is extremly fast, but also extremely clean too. It's very important you try to sound as clean as possible. No matter how fast you can play these exercises, if it doesn't sound clean then the exercise has not been played properly. Concentrate on sounding clean and at tempo.

Inside Picking & Outside Picking

Terms **Inside Picking** and **Outside Picking** refers on how we change from one string to another when using the alternate picking technique.

Outside Picking occurs when at changing from one string to another the pick stays **out** of both strings, see the next example:

Inside Picking occurs when at changing from one string to another the pick stays **between** of both strings, see the next example:

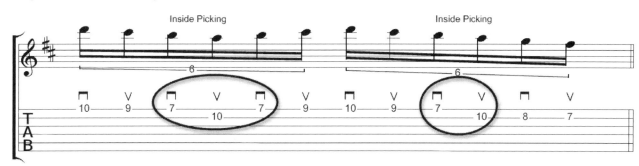

The major complication of the alternate picking technique is located precisely in the string changing. Passing from one string to another correctly it's commonly what generates more *technical difficulties*. These two are the only ways we can change from one string to another. The basic exercises will focus on both issues.

Paul Gilbert controls perfectly both ways of strings changing, but if he could choose he prefers **outside picking**. In fact, in the vast majority of his fast phrases the pick goes outside, but also he masters perfectly the inside picking.

Passing from one string to another using outside picking seems at first more complicated and slow, as it requires a larger movement from the right-hand. But once practised it's a very comfortable way of passing from one string to another, also we have more control over the accents. Anyway, **both ways have to be practised** and then we could spend more time in the exercises that focuses on the technique which results more complicated for us.

Made these clarifications let's get started with the basic exercises of **Paul Gilbert**, ordered from less to more difficulty.

1 Basic alternate picking sequence (**outside picking**).

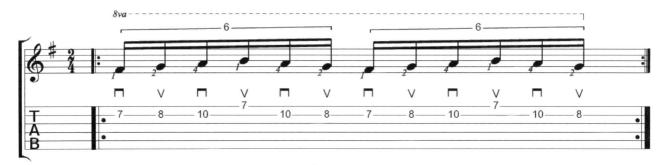

2 Basic alternate picking sequence (**inside picking**).

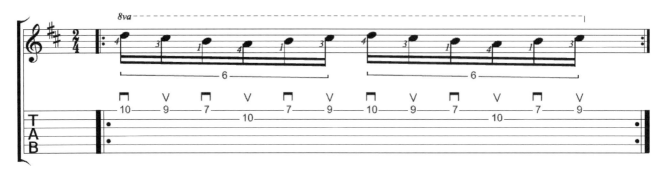

3 Quintuplet sequence. When played fast it could be played as a 10 notes in a row, making it an easier measure.

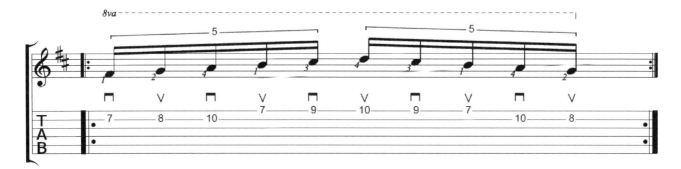

4 Similar to previous example, now with inside picking.

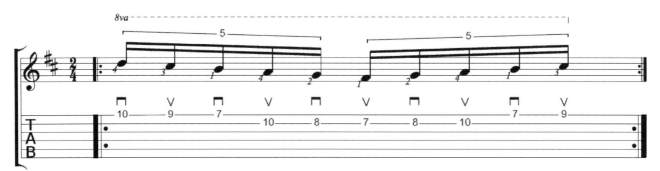

5 Alternate picking sequence with outside picking.

6 Similar to exercise 5, using inside picking.

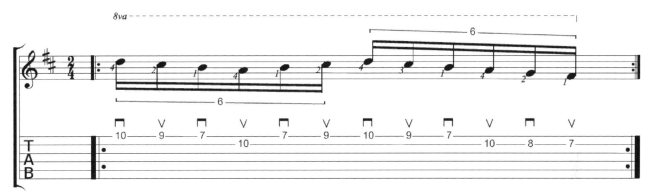

7 Ascending sequence of alternate picking in 16ths, you must concentrate in accenting every four notes.

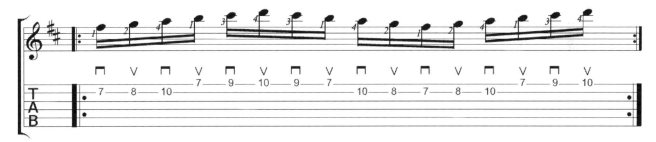

8 Same pattern as exercise 7, starting descending and with inside picking.

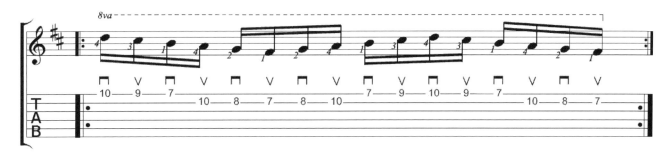

9 In this example we have another 16ths sequence with outside picking.

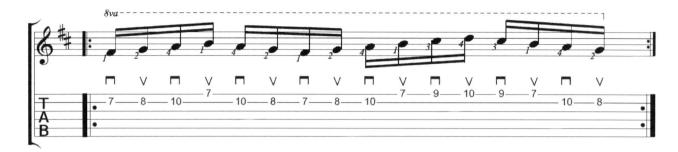

10 Similar as example 9, with inside picking.

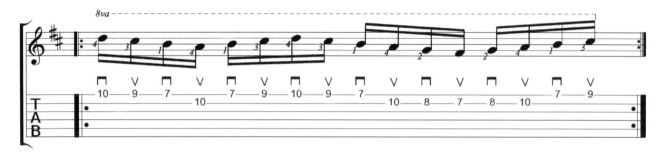

11 Ascending sequence in sextuplets with outside picking. This pattern is very easy so we could begin to increase the metronome speed.

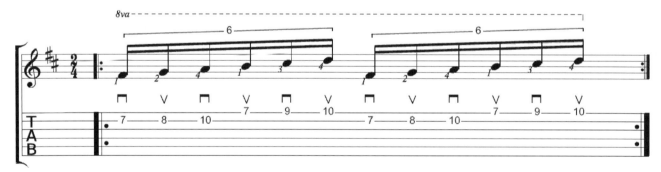

12 Sextuplet descending sequence.

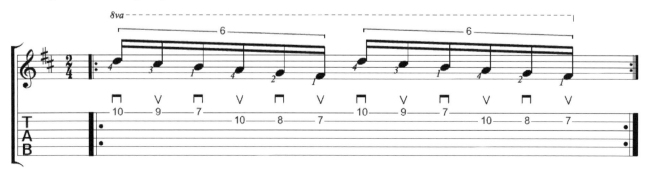

13 Next example is the same sequence as example 11. However, in this case we combine both alternate picking and legato. Even though it could seem difficult combining alternate picking with legato, once is mastered this kind of sequences are a lot easier to play than with strictly alternate picking.

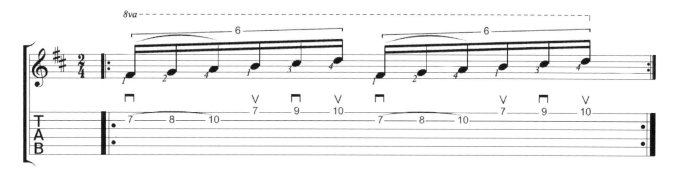

14 Descending sequence mixing alternate picking with legato. **Paul Gilbert** frequently uses this combination, we'll see it in depth later.

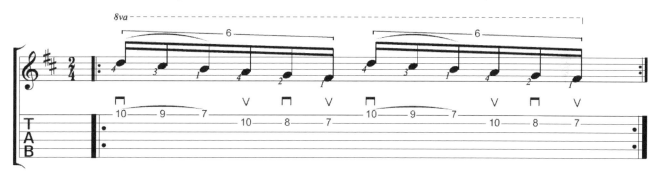

15 This exercise connects two patterns, ascends through one pattern and descends by the other.

Here it is the pattern used in example 15:

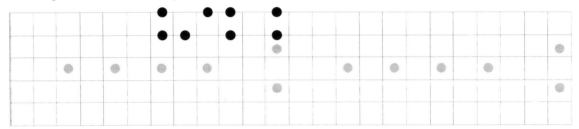

The same pattern from an intervallic point of view instead just "black dots", we can see the intervallic relationship with the tonic of **B minor** scale.

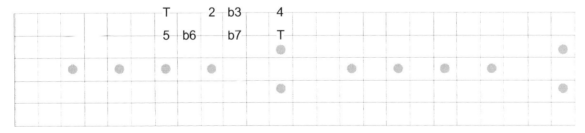

If you want to learn **Paul Gilbert**'s style you have to not only master the exercises and licks suggested in this book but know and control the patterns Paul uses too. Along this book we'll see his favourite patterns, shown with diagrams or drawings as the one we have just seen.

If we look carefully at the basic exercises, we've used always this two strings pattern:

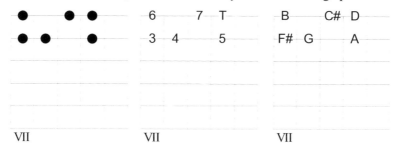

But it's not necessary to limit ourselves to that pattern, we could practice the previous sequences over any two-strings group if belongs to any scale.

For instance, these are two-strings sequences in **B minor** scale:

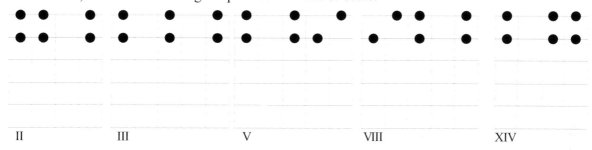

And here we have the complete pattern of **B minor** scale along two strings. You can practice the basic exercises over any six notes group and even move on horizontally over the pattern as we have seen in example #15.

B minor pattern in 2 strings

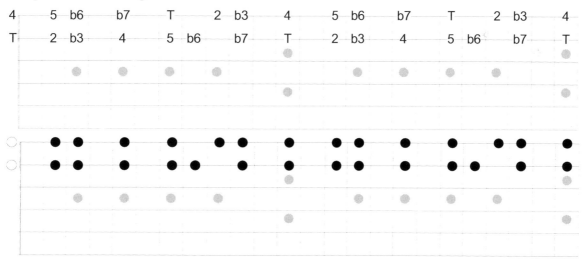

Pay attention to the sound

Pay special attention to the sound you achieve when practicing the exercises. I remember perfectly the first VHS video I bought from **Paul Gilbert**: **Intense Rock**. I could play the same exercises along the video with the same speed than Paul, but mine sounded totally different and I didn't know why. The answer was the accents. You have to try to accent every group of notes, it's not about just playing fast, groups must be properly accented so the "burst of notes" will be clearly defined, being these sextuplets, 16ths, quintuplets, etc.

Legato

In this section we'll see some exercises and examples based on legato technique. **Paul Gilbert** combines perfectly legato with alternate picking, these examples are a proof of it.

16 In this first exercise it's shown the basic alternate picking pattern of **Paul Gilbert** with no picking attack but the ones to pass from one string to the other.

This exercise can be played with two upstrokes (∨∨) making a little sweep, but **Paul Gilbert** <u>always</u> uses the combination upstroke/downstroke (∨⊓) in this kind of sequences.

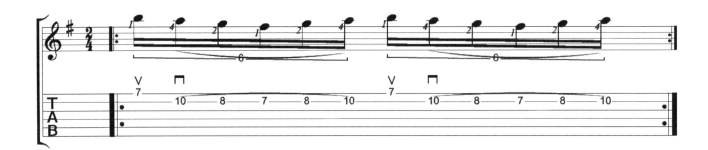

17 In this variation the most of the notes are in the first string instead of the second string. For this pattern **Paul** always uses the fingers 1 (index), 3 (ring) and 4 (pinky), but we can use fingers 1, 2 and 3, this one is my favourite fingering. In this case we could use two downstrokes (⊓⊓) but Paul prefers upstroke/downstroke for this sequence.

18 Next example combines the two previous patterns in **A Dorian** scale.

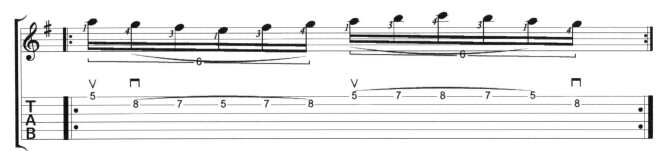

19 Here it is a similar approach as example 17. **Paul Gilbert** applies in several occasions this type of stuff over dorian and blues scales.

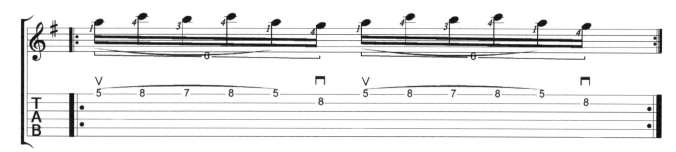

A Dorian scale pattern.

A Dorian scale pattern with blue note (b5).

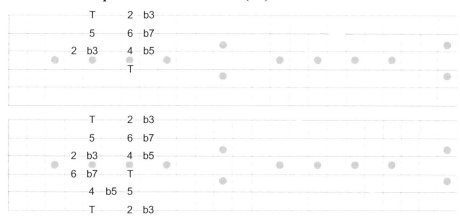

A Blues scale.

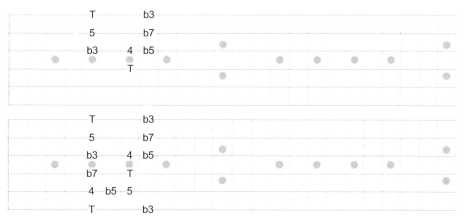

* The **Blue scale** is a **minor pentatonic** with a **blue note (b5)** added.

Further on, we'll see in depth **Paul Gilbert**'s favourite "scalar patterns".

20 In this example we use a diatonic pattern from **B minor** or **B frigian** scale (there is no 2nd interval , the mode is not defined) in 3 strings. In this case the value note is 16th.

Very often **Paul Gilbert uses this kind of pattern when playing 32nd notes.** Assuming a 90/130 BPM tempo, when soloing he may plays 16th sextuplets patterns with alternate picking and then this kind of pattern in 32nd notes with legato for the faster licks.

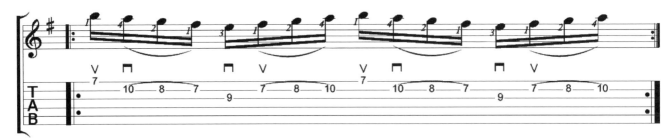

21 Similar sequence as the example above, in this case over an **A Dorian** pattern in which has been added the blue note.

22 A minimal but interesting variation of example #21. In this case we are moving between the notes of A and C in the high E string. Is not necessary to alternate always with these notes in the same order, we can create melodies or combinations of our liking.

23 Same idea as the previous exercise with a slight difficulty added. Paul is very fond of this sort of things.

24 Same concept in 16th notes and using 3 strings.

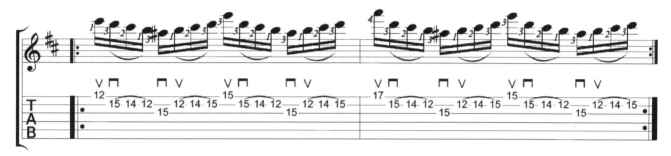

25 Similar style, now starting from the B string.

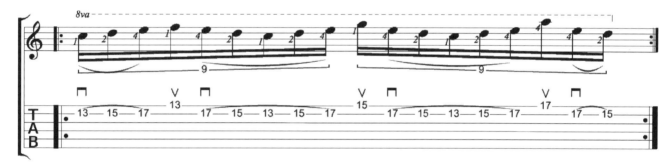

This example is a good alternate picking exercise too.

26 This one is another pattern frequently used by **Paul Gilbert**. This example uses a **B minor scale**, but he may applies that pattern on **pentatonics, blues scale** or **Dorian scale with the blue note**.

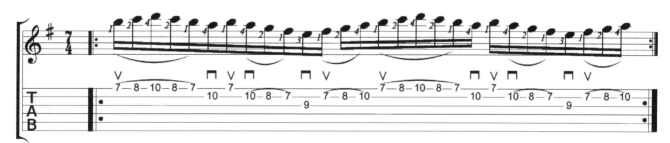

27 Here we can see the pattern from the previous example, in this case in **B dorian with the blue note** (b5). **This scale** (not necessarily in this key), **is whithout a doubt one of Paul Gilbert's favourites.**

Note the metric difference, which it's easier to internalize, simply we need to concentrate on playing as fast as we can and accent properly the first pattern note.

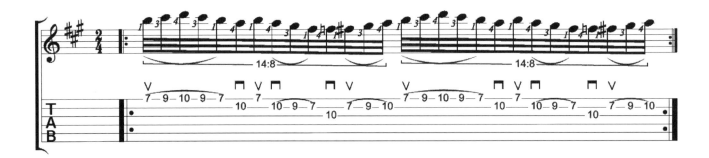

The fingering used by Gilbert is 1, 3 and 4 prescinding the middle finger in every moment (it's the annotated fingering). I preffer the 1, 2, 3 fingering and there is no sound variaton to me so feel free to use the fingering most comfortable to you, or even I would recommend 1, 2, 3 fingering for working on left hand stretches.

28 **This pattern is one of Paul's favorite too.** The interesting thing it's the value notes and the off-beat created in the second beat. It's without a doubt something that Gilbert likes to use very often, I think I've never heard any improvised solo from him in which he didn't use this rhythmic resource.

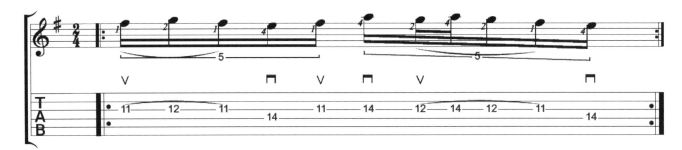

When the lowest string in a pattern is a wound string Paul tries always to mute it with his right hand to make a more percussive feel, so if you want to emulate his sound you should make it too.

29 Same sequences as previous, in **E minor scale** too but in the high strings.

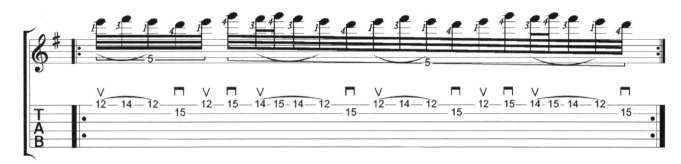

30 Here we have a variation from the previous example in which we play the same pattern but utilizing an **A blues scale.**

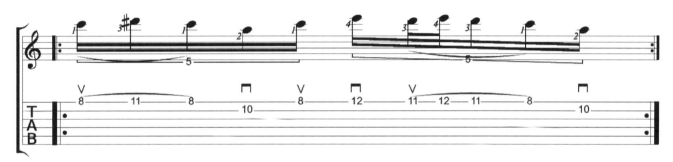

A blues scale

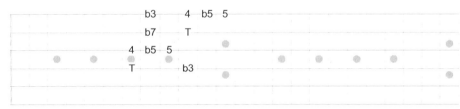

A blues scale (complete pattern)

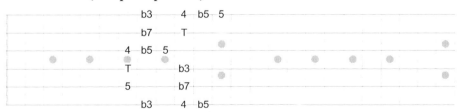

* The **Blues Scale** is a **minor pentatonic** with a **blue note** (b5) added.

31 In this example we can see a 32nd notes pattern which we can play it very fast without too many technical difficulties.

32 Another phrase with the previous pattern, this one in 3 strings and using **A Dorian scale with the blue note**.

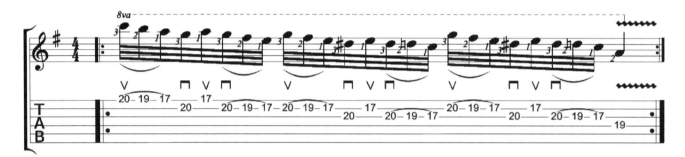

With no doubt this is one of the Gilbert's favourite scale.

33 Same idea as exercise 32 developed over the whole scale and in a lower octave.

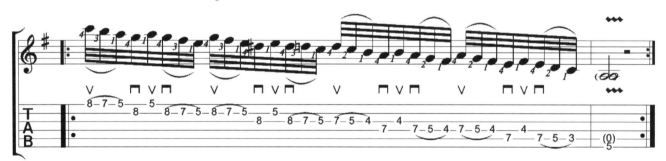

A Dorian scale with the Blue note (b5)

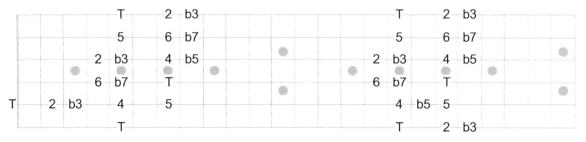

Legato and Pentatonics

In this section we will see how **Paul Gilbert** uses legato over classic pentatonic patterns.

It's very important to use the stroke direction as indicated in every example. Maybe at first it would be easier for you to play it in another way, but if you want to achieve the tone of **Paul Gilbert**, and with the practice maybe being able to play these patterns as him, there's no other way than using the right hand (up and down strokes) the same way **Paul** does.

34 Pentatonic pattern in triplets. Try to mute a bit the fourth string with your right hand.

35 B minor pentatonic along the higher strings.

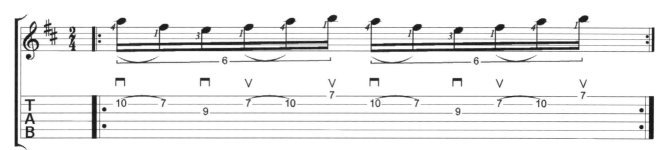

36 B minor pentatonic with the **blue note** and alternating the first string note.

Paul Gilbert uses this idea alternating the first string note with the blue note, in this case would be between the notes F (blue note) and E. An example of this is shown in exercise 40.

37 Complete **B minor pentatonic** scale, ascending pattern.

38 Complete **B minor pentatonic** scale, descending pattern.

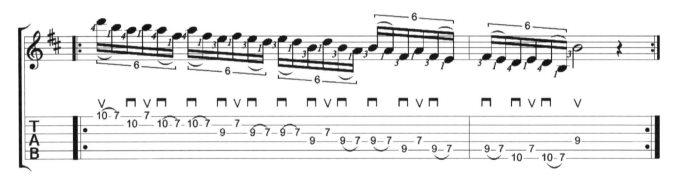

Actually this way of playing pentatonics is not typical of **Gilbert**. Paul often uses patterns of three notes per string to play descending pentatonics, but as an exercise I put this pattern also in descending form.

B minor pentatonic

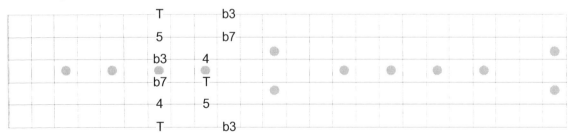

39 B minor pentatonic. Basic 16th pattern.

40 B minor pentatonic with the **blue note**.

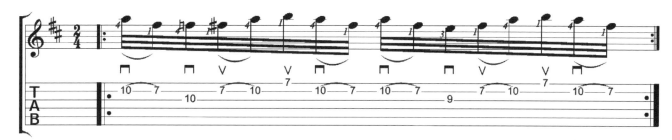

41 Similar to the previous example but modifying the high note, mind the effect created.

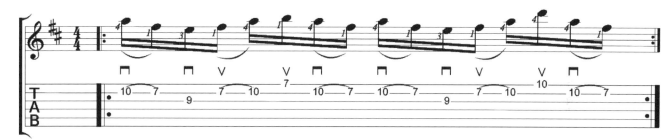

42 Complete **B minor pentatonic**, ascending.

23

43 As seen with the triplets patterns, Paul doesn't use very often the classic pattern for the minor pentatonic scale when descending. But as an exercise, we can use this pattern to practice legato over the **minor pentatonic** in sixteenths.

B blues scale

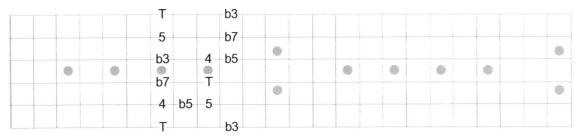

* The **blues scale** is a **minor pentatonic** with a **blue note (b5)** added.

44 Here we have a different sequence, it's in **D minor pentatonic** with an added **blue note**.

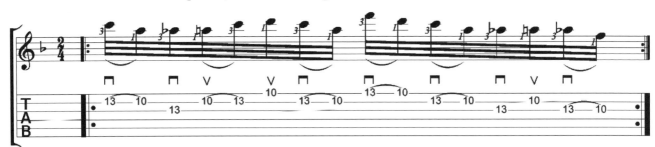

D minor pentatonic with an added blue note (b5), or **D blues scale**.

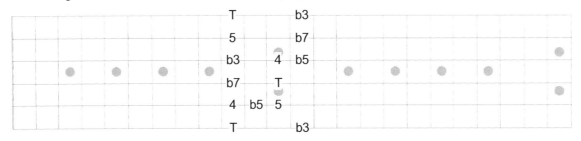

24

45 The following one is a **D blues scale** in a not common pattern for the majority of guitarists, but so familiar to **Paul Gilbert.**

D blues scale

Favorite patterns, scales and sequences of Paul Gilbert

Paul Gilbert uses very often patterns of 3 notes per string. We could say, without the shadow of a doubt, that patterns of 3 notes per strings over any scale are their favorites. No matter what the scale is, diatonic, pentatonic, symmetrical, he even uses the 3 notes per string pattern with the arpeggios as we will see further.

We are going to concentrate on diatonic scales, in the next example we will see all the 3 notes per string pattern derived from **C major** scale.

Notice that we have two patterns for each position, the first one will show the intervallic formula, the second only the pattern itself. I preffer to see the scale intervals but I keep in mind that maybe it's easier to just memorize the pattern.

C major scale pattern, 3 notes per string, beginning in the fourth note of the scale.

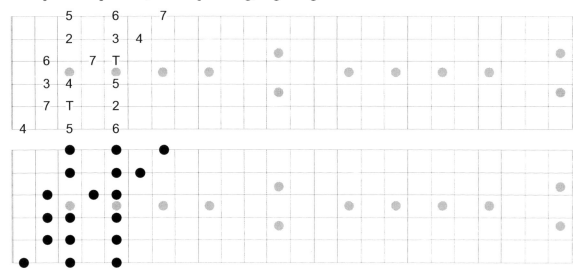

C major scale beginning from the fifth note.

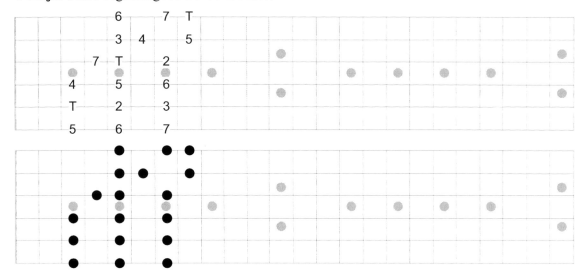

C major scale from the sixth note.

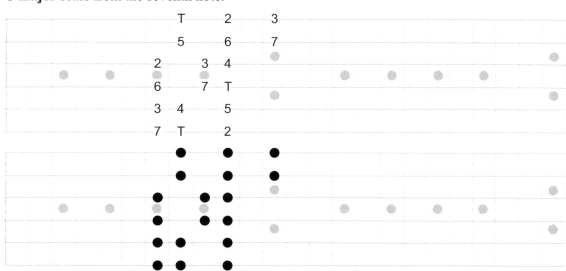

C major scale from the seventh note.

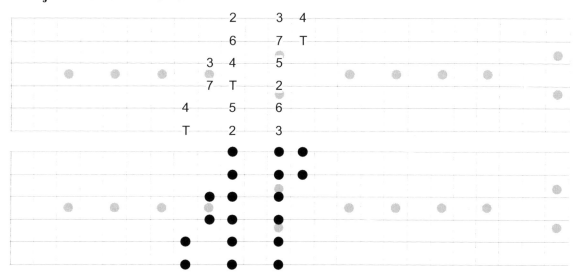

C major scale from the tonic.

C major scale from the second note.

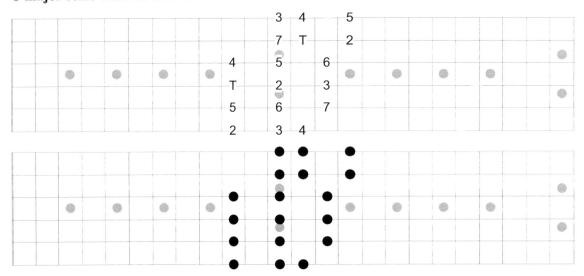

C major scale from the third note.

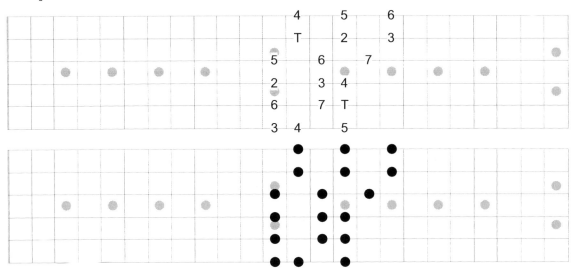

In these patterns, we have seen the 7 possible combinations of 3 notes per string pattern in **C major scale**, **Paul Gilbert** perfectly masters these patterns in every key. However, I must say the keys he most uses are **C major** (or the relative, A minor), **G major** (or E minor), **D major** (or B minor), **A major** (or F# minor) and **E major** (or C# minor).

If you need to study the patterns in the traditional way you could start in that particular order, you will notice there is only one different note from each one. For instance, C major have no accidentals, G major have only one, which is F#, D major have two accidentals, F# and C#.

So we must memorize and practice all the patterns in every single key. The following examples are in **C major** but should be practiced in every pattern and key.

3 notes per string sequences

46 In this example we have an alternate picking sequence of **3 notes per string in C major.**

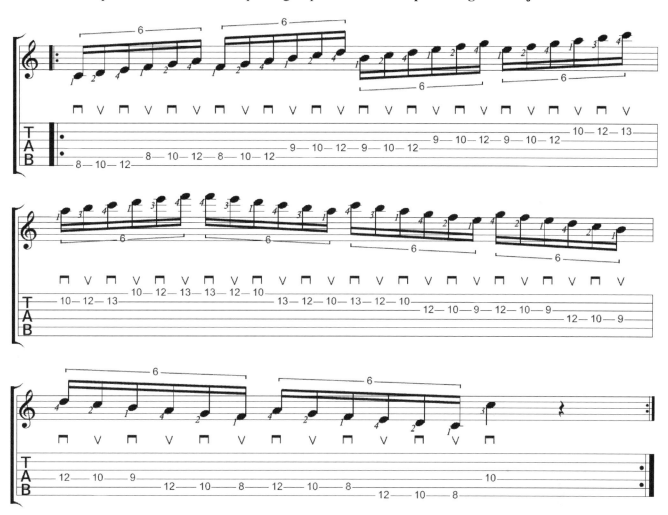

This kind of sequences are typical of **Paul Gilbert's** style, and are used by many other guitarists too, **John Petrucci** is one of them.

47 Next sequence mixes alternate picking with legato. Once we achieve both right and left hand coordination it becomes easier than the previous exercise.

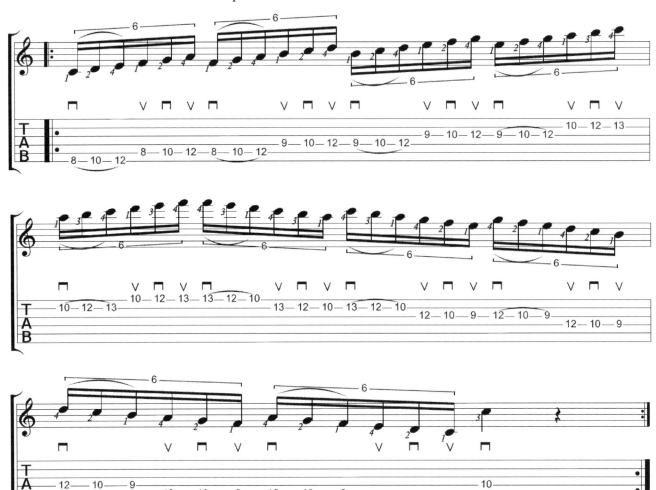

48 Alternate picking sequence in **C major using a 3 notes per string pattern.**

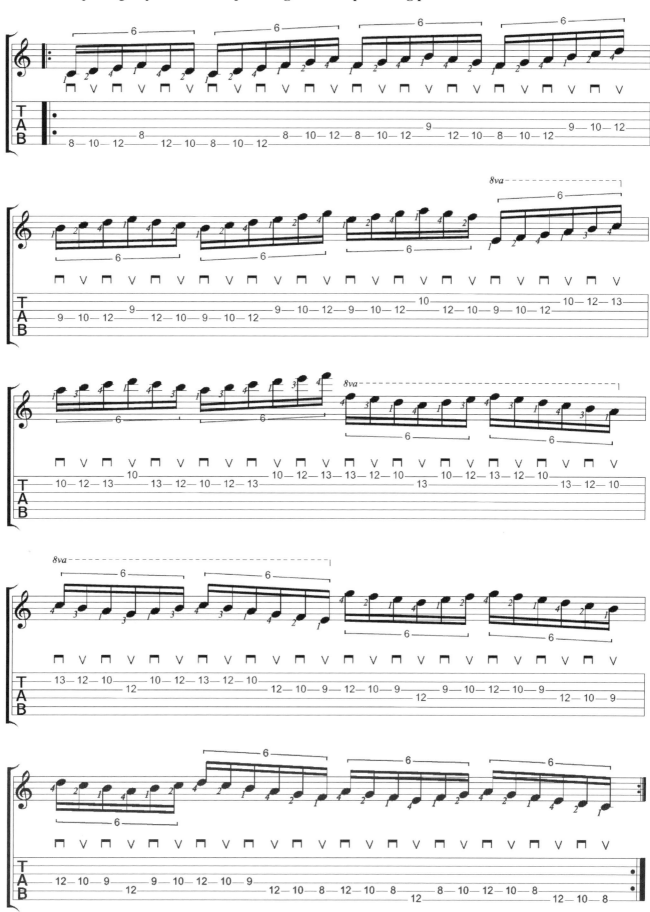

The sequence in exercise 48 is the essence of **Paul Gilbert**'s technique. It's a sequence we saw in the first basic exercises, but now is developed over the whole scale, that makes it significantly harder. Anyway, and aside of the speed we can play it, it's a very good alternate picking exercise so we should practice it with attention and constancy.

49 Paul Gilbert uses very often this resource, it's the junction of two patterns of 3 notes per string. This allows **Gilbert** to move horizontally through the entire neck passing from one pattern to the next. In this example we will concentrate in the first four strings.

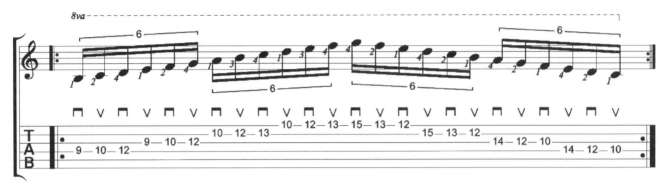

Notice how we've connected two patterns.

One pattern when ascending:

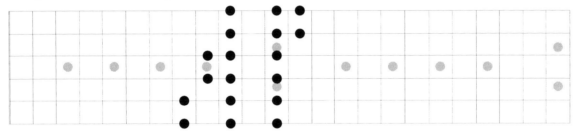

And next pattern when descending:

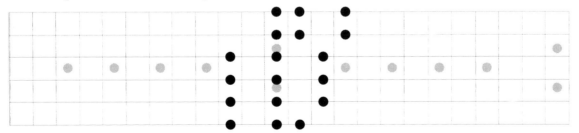

50 Same idea as exercise 49 but in this case over the six strings, we use the complete patterns so maybe it's a bit more complex.

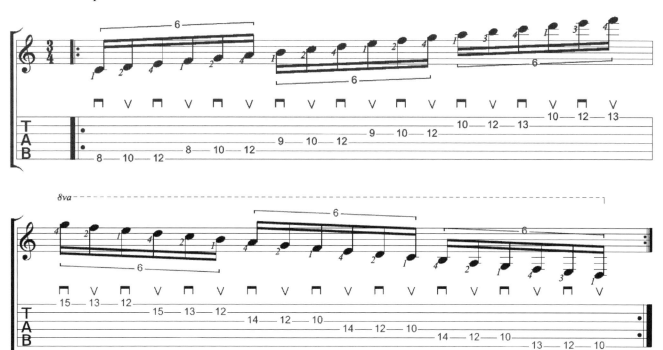

To accomplish a true complete work in this pattern's study, you could practice every examples seen till this point **ascending through one pattern and descending through the next**, as seen in exercises 49 and 50, applying the sequences shown at 46, 47 and 48.

For a better control and knowledge of the 3 notes per string patterns don't limit yourself to the pattern's junction seen in example 5, practice every sequence seen till the moment, and the following, over any pattern and key.

Patterns and sequences in 2 strings

Another scalar patterns typical of **Gilbert** are the 2 strings patterns. These patterns allow to develop all kind of sequences ascending and descending. **Paul Gilbert** uses these sequences very often through the entire neck.

The following examples will show exercises and sequences developed in 2 strings.

This is the 2 strings pattern we will use in the following examples, in **E minor.**

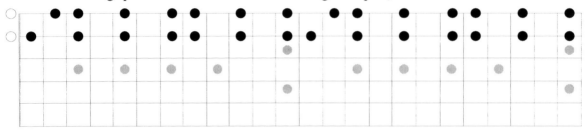

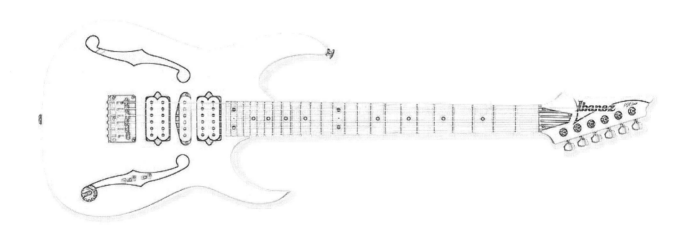

51 First sequence combines alternate picking with legato, you can practice it with **only alternate picking or legato** too.

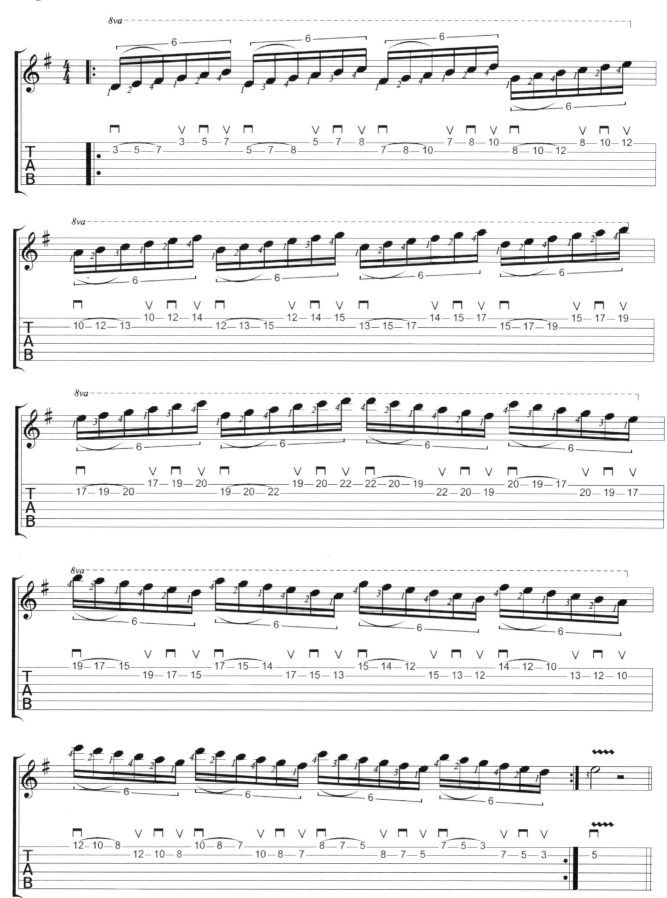

52 This is a sequence of alternate picking in **E minor**. **Paul Gilbert** uses a lot this kind of sequence.

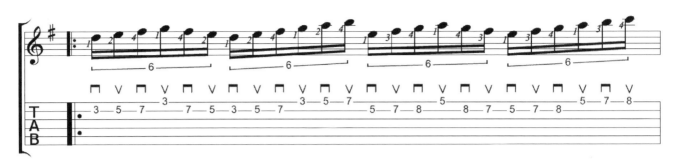

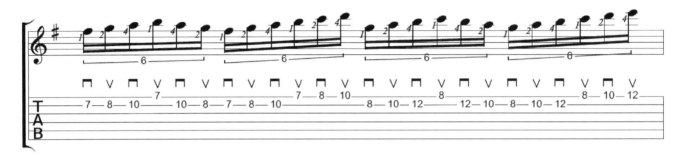

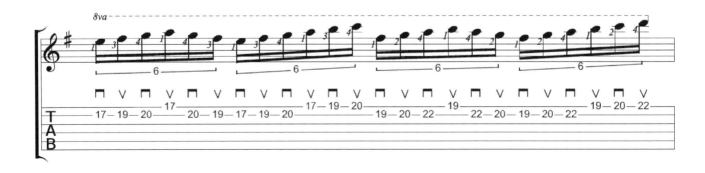

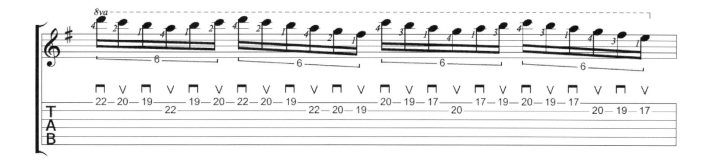

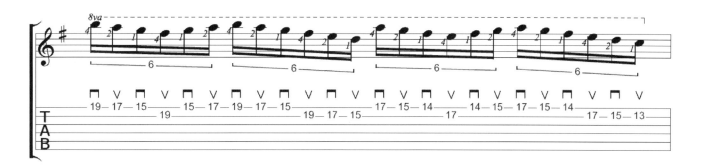

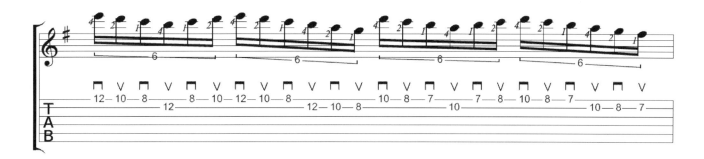

53 Another typical sequence of **Paul Gilbert**, this time we play in sixteenths.

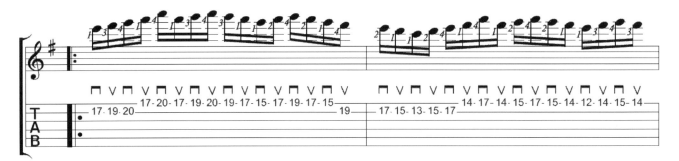

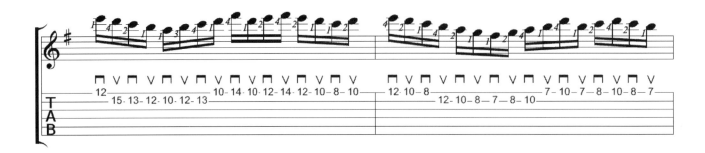

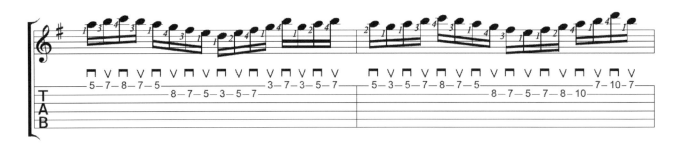

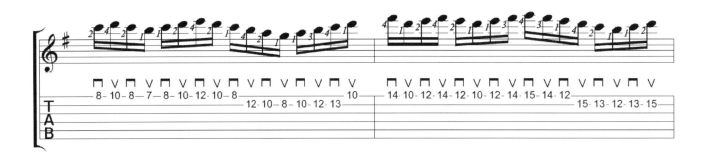

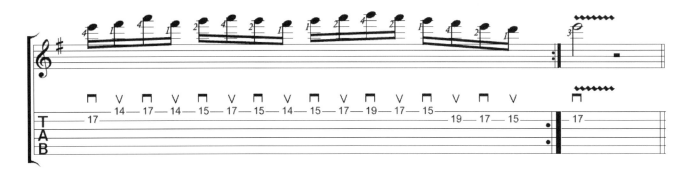

54 Paul Gilbert masters every group of two strings, but his favorites are 1ˢᵗ and 2ⁿᵈ, 3ᵗʰ and 4ᵗʰ.

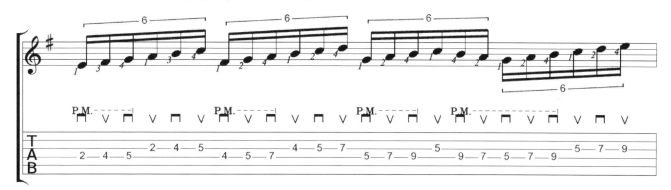

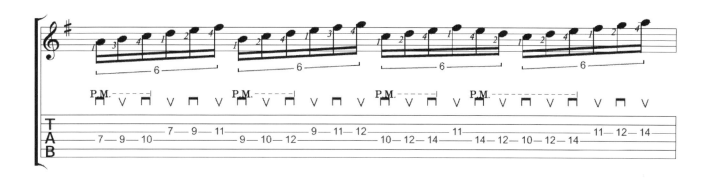

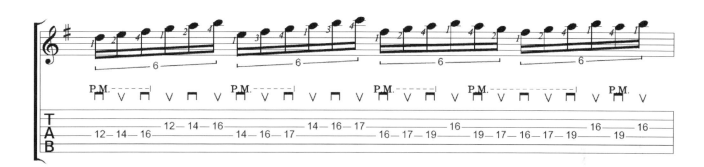

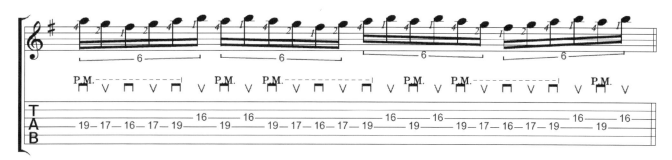

Usually when **Gilbert** plays on wounded strings he tries to mute it with his right hand palm, that's the "palm muting" technique, by this way is achieved a more percussive sound and a cleaner definition.

Here we have the **E minor** pattern **in strings 3ᵗʰ and 4ᵗʰ**.

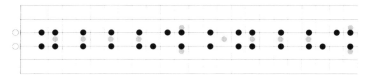

Dorian scale, Dorian with the Blue note, and the hybrid scale

Possibly the dorian mode is the favorite of **Paul Gilbert**.

A very common pattern of this scale or mode could be this one:

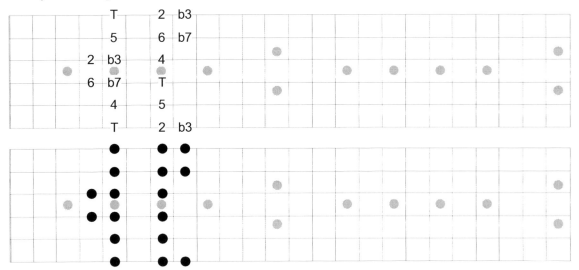

55 Paul Gilbert uses very often the dorian scale pattern. In this exercise we have a sequence which mixes alternate picking with legato over the pattern we have just seen.

Here is a variation of **A Dorian scale**, same notes as the previous pattern but differently ordered.

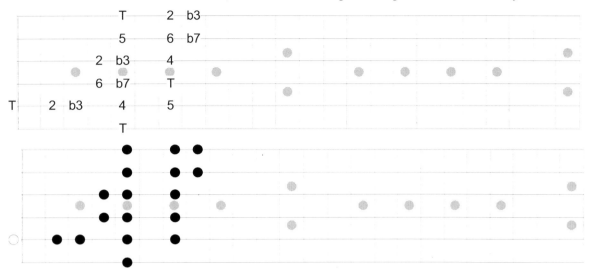

This variation is especially useful when we want to start or finish with an opened A string.

Many times Paul adds the blue note in the dorian scale.

This is **A Dorian scale with the blue note** pattern.

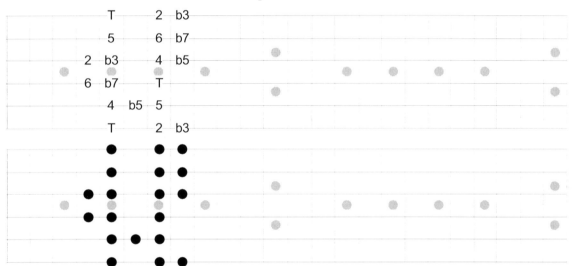

56 We have seen to this point the dorian scale with a blue note in little phrases, less than an octave. The next example shows a sequence reaching two octaves of the scale.

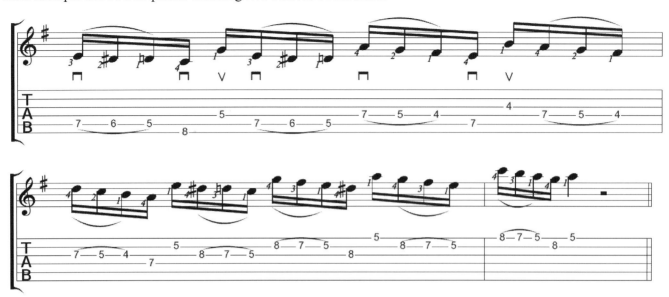

¿What would happen if we mix 2 of the Gilbert's favorite scales?

These scales would be **minor pentatonic** and **dorian scale** with the blue note, the result it's what we could name the **hybrid scale of Gilbert.**

This is the **Hydrid scale pattern in A minor**:

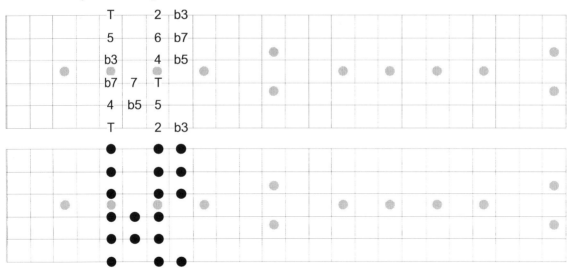

The hybrid scale mixes the minor pentatonic and the Dorian mode with the blue note.

You may notice in this pattern that there is a note which is not from minor pentatonic nor dorian mode.

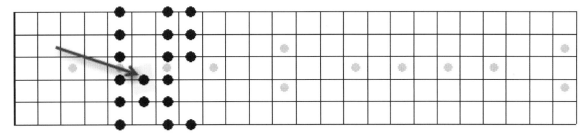

Is a G# and it doesn't matter it's out of key, we should play this note as a chromaticism, so it will sound good any time we don't finish our phrases on it.

The aim of this note is to achieving a pattern with 3 notes per string.

57 The following example is a descending phrase of the **hybrid scale** in **A minor.**

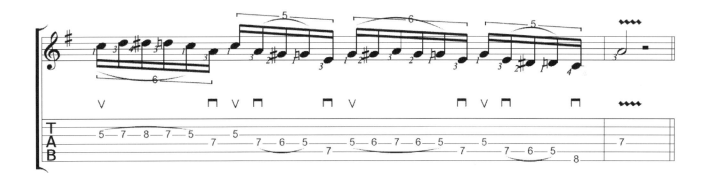

This scale contains 3 notes per string, so you could apply any of the exercises #46, #47 and #48 to this pattern.

Scales in diagonal

So far we have seen how Paul Gilbert moves through the neck vertically by patterns of 3 notes per string, also we have seen horizontally with scalar patterns and sequences developed in two strings.

Now we will see how he moves diagonally in patterns of 3 and 4 notes per string.

E minor scale in a pattern of 3 and 4 notes per string, **ascending**.

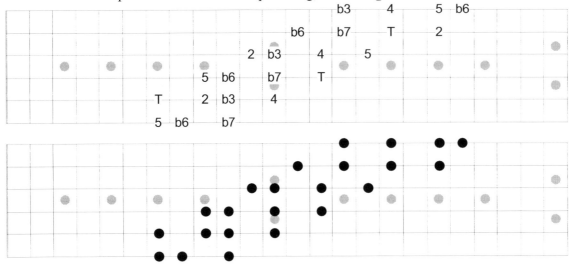

Notice how the resultant drawing shows a diagonal displacement, is because of the 3 and 4 notes per string. If we had only 3 notes per string the displacement it would be vertical.

58 In this example we have sextuplets with alternate picking, same pattern than previous exercise.

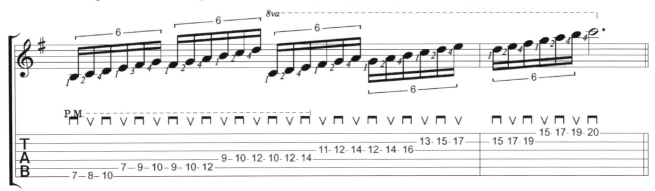

This one is a classic of **Paul Gilbert**, also keep in mind it's not exclusive himself, many modern guitarists use this kind of ideas and patterns.

59 Same idea, now **descending.**

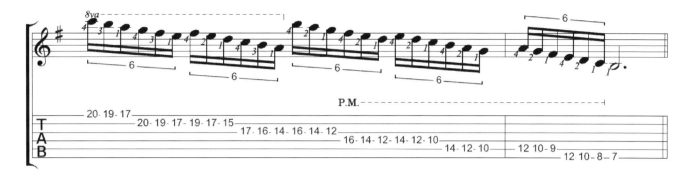

Notice that playing this pattern descending, the strings which contained 3 notes now contains 4 and viceversa. Here is an **E minor scale** in a descending diagonal pattern.

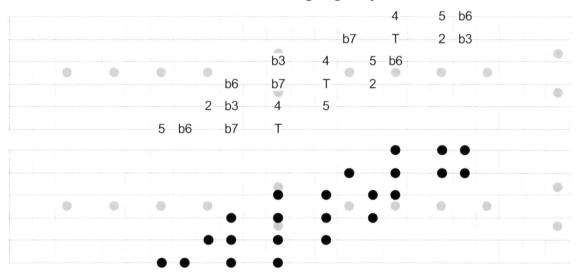

60 The following exercise is an **ascending sequence** with alternate picking over a diagonal pattern, this case is a sequence of 32th notes.

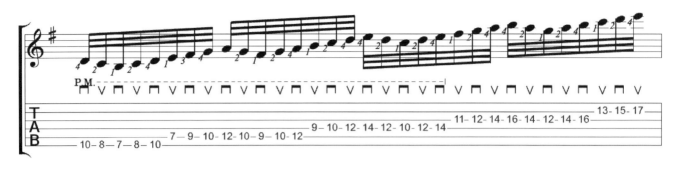

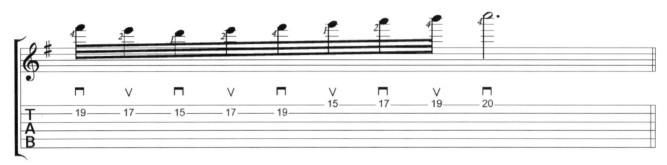

61 Same idea but **descending**.

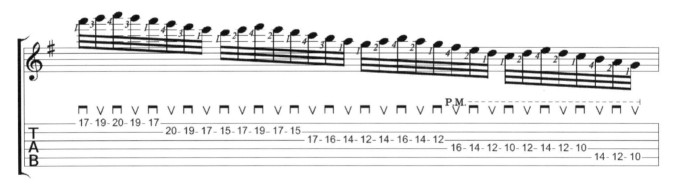

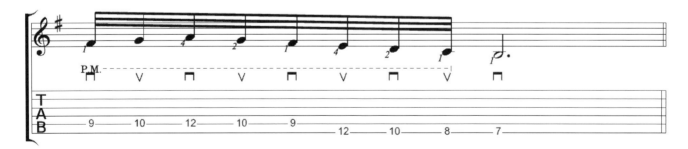

Harmonic minor scale

Paul Gilbert masters perfectly this scale, but it's not one he would use a lot. Even seems like he tries to avoid it to not sound too much as **Malmsteen**, who abused of it and these days anything played fast in the harmonic minor scale sounds like him.

Yngwie was a huge influence for **Paul Gilbert**, to the point that **Paul** learned every single song from "Rising force" (first LP of **Yngwie Malmsteen**). Maybe the young Paul didn't have the talent and freshness **Malmsteen** had, but he had the courage and perseverance to become the most technical and perfect guitarist of the period. Further on he would show his abilities and musicianship with great songs in **Racer X**, and he would create some phrases and licks with which he would be instantly recognized. His character and charisma would do the rest to succeed and got the rightful place and recognition he deserves in the history of the electric guitar.

Paul has really used only a few patterns of the **harmonic minor scale**, this is one of them:

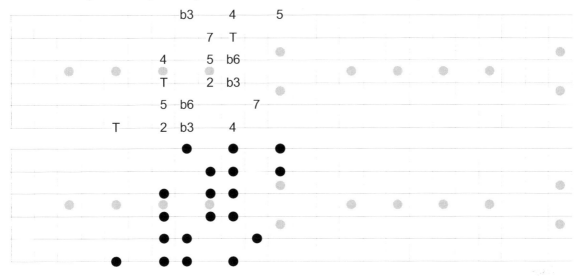

Gilbert masters at perfection the other six patterns of the harmonic minor scale in three notes per string. If you like how it sounds it would be a great idea to learn it too.

Rest of patters of **A Harmonic Minor**:

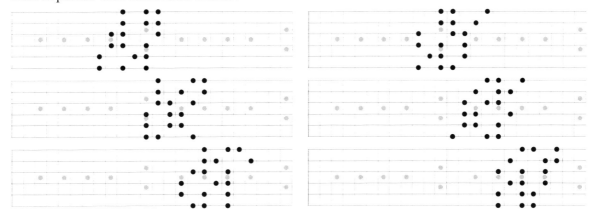

62 In contrast to **Malmsteen**, who mixes alternate picking and legato in his phrases with this scale, **Paul Gilbert** can play it with estrictly alternate picking with no effort, but the result is always the same, a sound that will remind us of **Malmsteen.**

In this example we see a phrase with the **harmonic minor scale of A**.

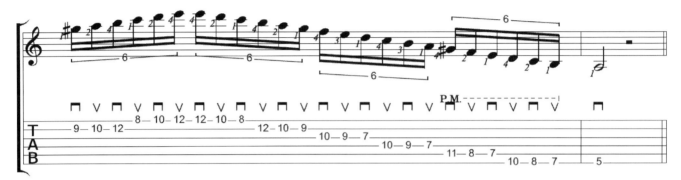

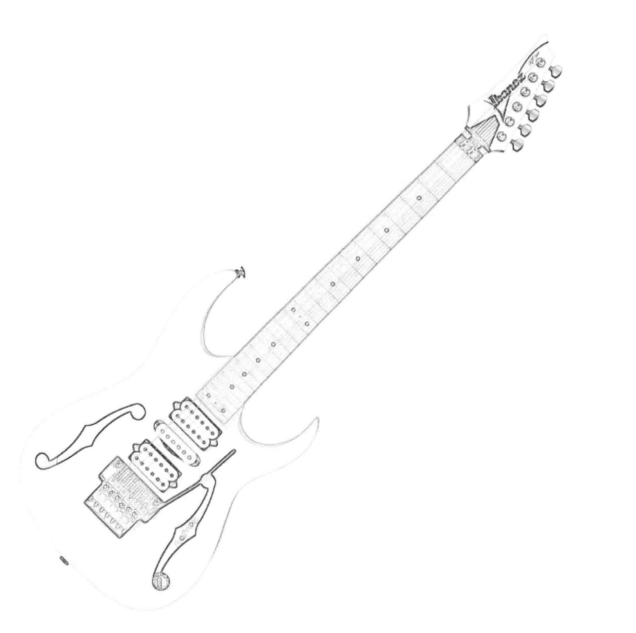

Symmetrical Patterns

Paul Gilbert uses **symmetrical patterns** every now and then.

The symmetrical patterns have a particularity, fingering is always the same for the left hand. This could be very useful in order to concentrate better in the right hand. In this section we will see some of the favorite symmetrical patterns of **Paul Gilbert.**

On occasions he uses this **symmetrical pattern** of **A harmonic minor** when ascending.

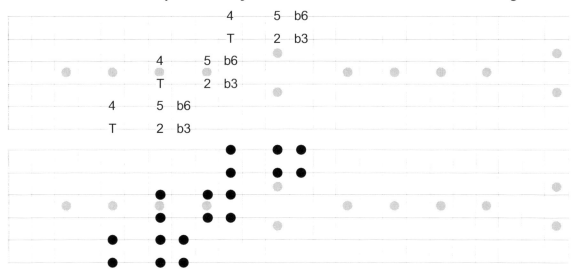

63 The following example shows an **ascending sequence** over the same pattern of **A harmonic minor.**

We have seen the former pattern so we know that he uses it to ascend through the scale, here we have the pattern he uses when **descending**.

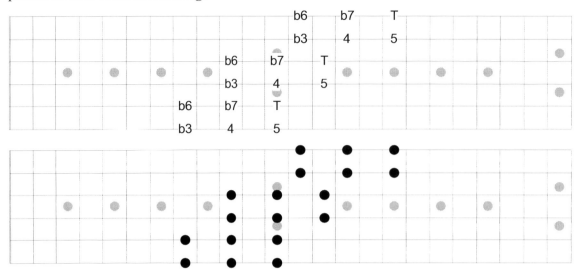

64 Descending sequence utilizing the previous pattern.

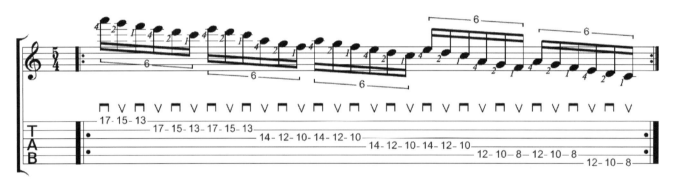

The complete pattern (ascending + descending) would be as follows:

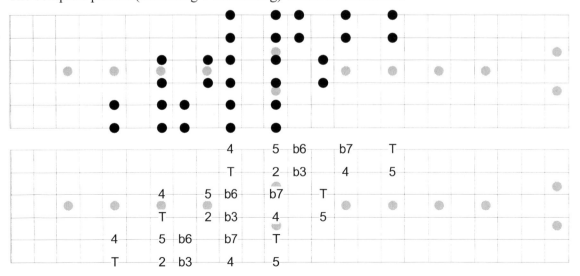

65 If we play the ascending pattern and then the descending one, the result will be this example.

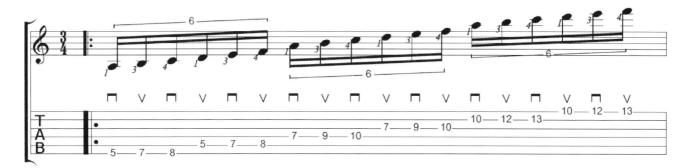

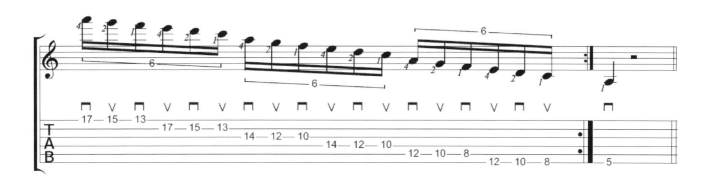

66 Here we have the same sequence, in this case mixing alternate picking with legato. As we have seen previously, **Paul Gilbert** likes to use sequences and phrases combining both techniques, as this example shows.

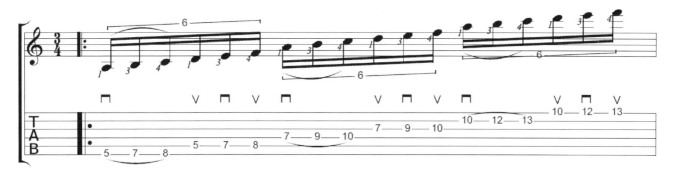

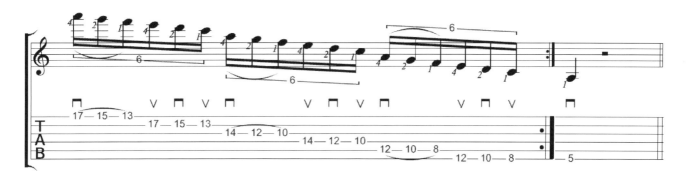

With the **blues scale** we can also make **symmetrical patterns of 3 notes per string**. Here we have the favorite symmetrical pattern of **Paul Gilbert** for the **blues scale**.

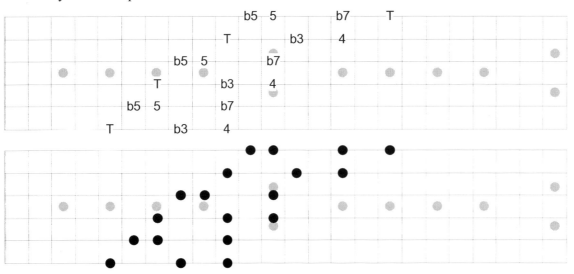

* The **blues scale** is a **minor pentatonic** with an added **blue note (b5)**.

67 This example shows an ascending and descending sequence with the **blues scale** using a **symmetrical pattern** of 3 notes per string.

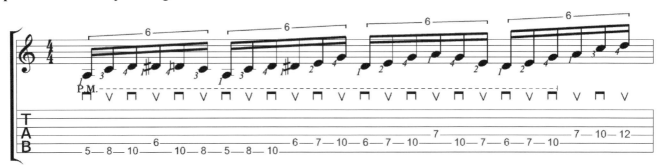

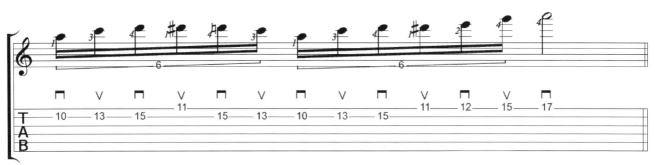

52

68 The same sequence, now descending.

You may have noticed that symmetrical patterns contains a total of six notes. Making a symmetrical pattern of 3 notes per string using a complete scale of 7 notes is not easy (is impossible). Ok, this is not a problem … we just take off one note and as a result we obtain symmetrical patterns of six strings. Having six notes instead seven will not define any mode but almost, and not defining a mode it's an advantage because we could use the same pattern in different keys or modes. **Paul Gilbert** knows pretty well this resource and he takes advantage of it fantastically.

Let's see some symmetrical pattern examples which have been taken off one note of its scale.

A minor scale without the sixth

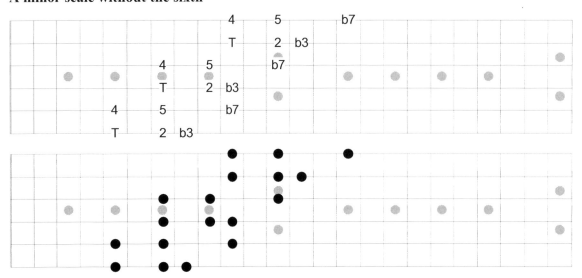

Because of the sixth's omission it can be used in the **Aeolian and Dorian modes.**

69 **Alternate picking** sequence using **A minor scale without the sixth**

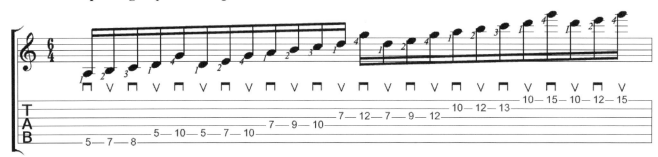

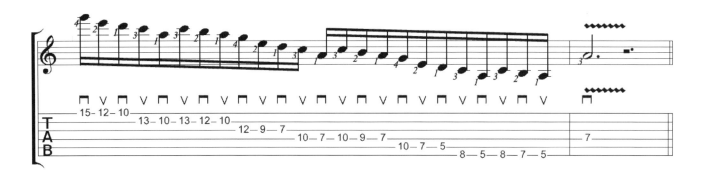

G major scale without seventh

For the following pattern **Paul Gilbert** uses the fingers 1, 2 and 4 of his left hand. This symmetrical pattern has a major third, so it's a major scale, the perfect fourth signifies that is not a Lydian mode (which contains an augmented fourth), the seventh's omission don't define any mode.

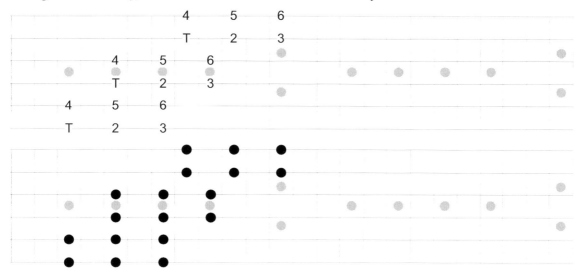

With the seventh's omission we can use this pattern in both **Mixolydian and Ionian modes.**

70 A legato example over the pattern we have just seen.

You can practice this example with alternate picking too.

String skipping

To this point we have seen different techniques, scales, and sequences that defines the style of **Paul Gilbert**. Even though every single thing we have seen are frequently used by **Paul Gilbert** none of them are exclusive or invented by him, however we could say that Paul took these techniques and sequences to another level.

In this section we will see **string skipping**, and this time we could say that almost every idea and sequences are invention of **Paul Gilbert.**

Triad arpeggios with string skipping (root in 4th string)

This is the favorite way of playing arpeggios for **Paul Gilbert. Paul masters perfectly the sweep picking technique**, however he rarely would use it.

In the 80's sweep picking was a technique used by every single virtuoso, Paul didn't want to sound as **Yngwie Malmsteen** or anyone else. **Paul Gilbert** knew that a great guitarist needs his own tone and his own techniques, so he decided to look for a different way of playing arpeggios. He developed the **string skipping technique**.

In the following examples we will see the patterns that **Paul** uses to play **triad arpeggios with string skipping**, also we will see **different metrics and sequences** he frequently uses.

La púa favorita de Paul Gilbert

71 This is the pattern for **major triad arpeggios** with string skipping (root in 4th string).

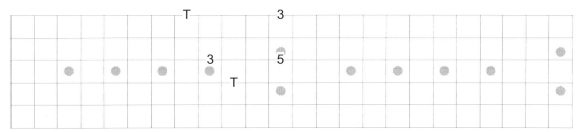

The next example shows how to play this pattern **ascending** and **descending**, using **sixteenth and sextuplets notes**, these are the metrics that **Paul** uses very often.

Is very important to pay attention to the pick strokes, play upstroke or downstroke wherever is indicated.

Sixteenth note sequence of C major:

Sextuplet note sequence of C major:

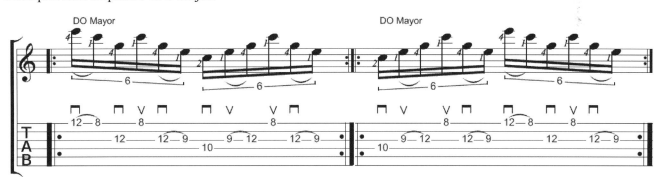

Some guitarists, as **Joey Tafolla**, use this kind of **arpeggios with string skipping** but modifying the pick strokes. **Joey**, for instance, makes two downstrokes when passing from the 4th string to the 3th, instead of an upstroke and then downstroke as this example shows. This is what **Paul Gilbert** does.

In this example we have seen the major pattern for major triads arpeggios with string skipping, in the followings we will see the rest: **minor, diminished and augmented arpeggios.**

72 Minor triad arpeggio pattern with string skipping (root in 4th string).

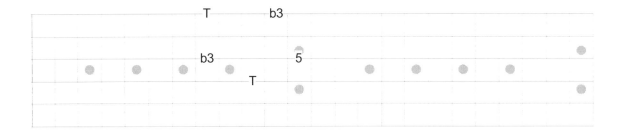

Sixteenth note sequence of C minor:

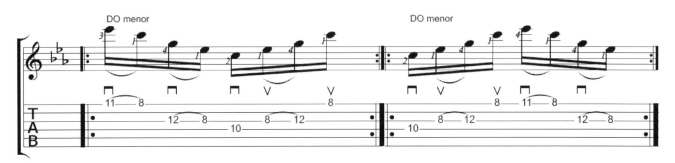

Sextuplet note sequence of C minor:

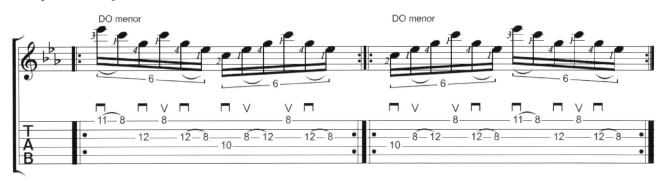

73 Diminished triad arpeggio pattern with string skipping (root in 4th string).

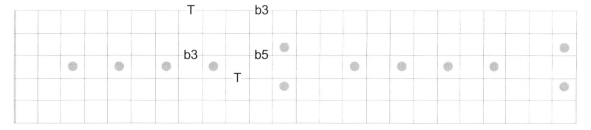

Sixteenth note sequence of C diminished:

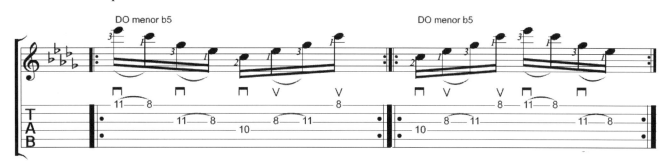

Sextuplet note pattern of C diminished:

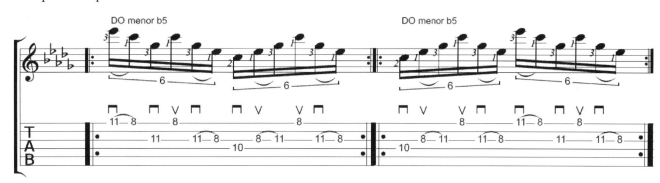

74 Augmented triad arpeggio pattern with string skipping (root in 4th string).

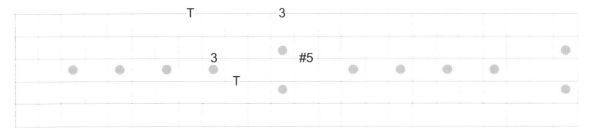

Sixteenth note sequence of C augmented:

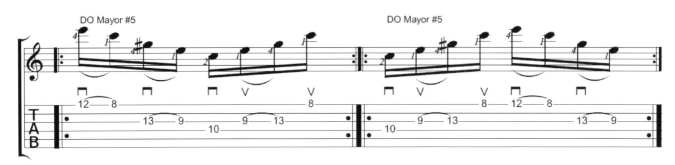

Sextuplet note sequence of C augmented:

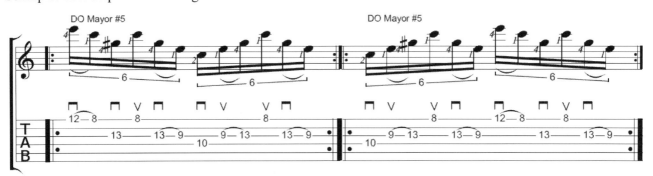

Triad arpeggios with string skipping (root in 5th string)

In this section we will focus on the same idea, **triad arpeggios with string** skipping, now with the root in the 5th string. Let's see the different patterns and sequences.

75 **Major triad arpeggio pattern** with string skipping (root in 5th string).

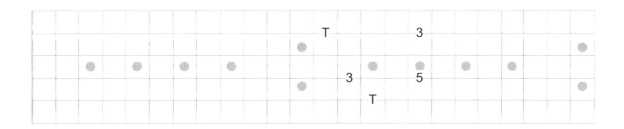

Sixteenth note sequence of C major:

Sextuplet note sequence of C major:

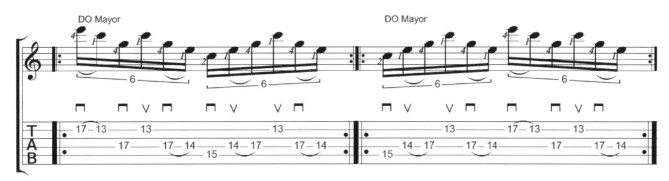

76 Minor triad arpeggio pattern with string skipping (root in 5th string).

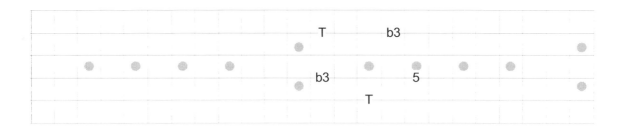

Sixteenth note sequence of C minor:

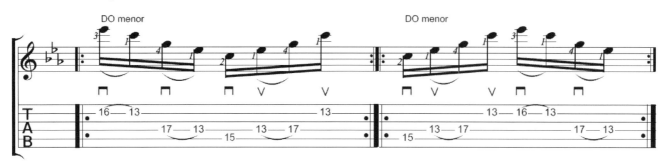

Sextuplet note sequence of C minor:

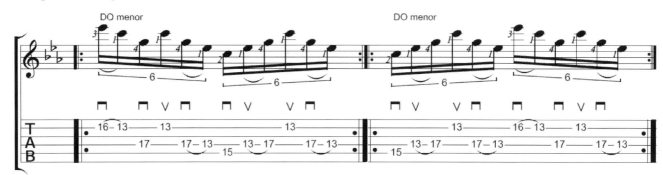

77 Diminished triad arpeggio pattern with string skipping (root in 5th string)

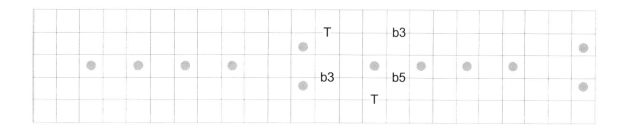

Sixteenth note sequence of C diminished:

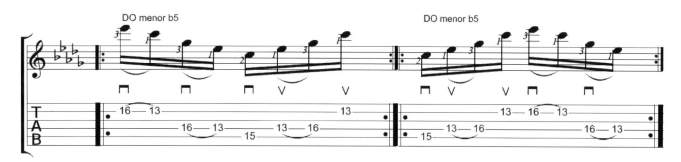

Sextuplet note sequence of C diminished:

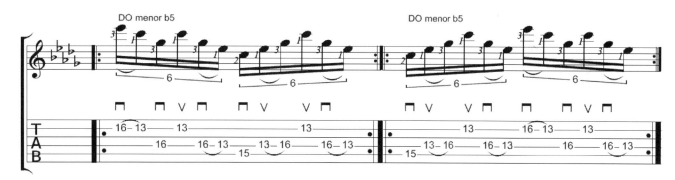

78 **Augmented triad arpeggio pattern** with string skipping (root in 5th string).

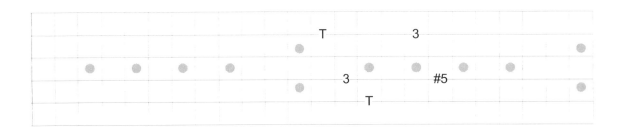

Sixteenth note sequence of C augmented:

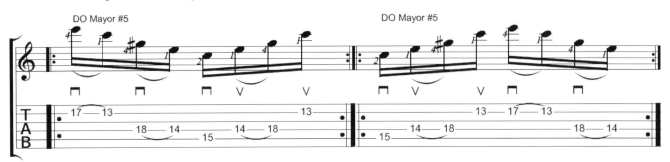

Sextuplet note sequence of C augmented:

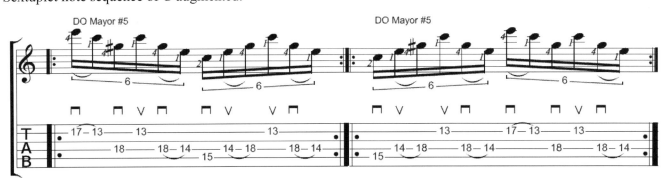

You may have noticed that the position is always the same, don't matter where the root is. This is a good point to memorize these patterns.

Studies with triad arpeggios and string skipping

The following exercises are two harmonic progressions in which we will play exclusively **arpeggios with string skipping**.

Practicing these studies will be a funny and effective manner of controlling and improving our technique.

But first, make sure you've practiced enough all the patterns shown till this point. In these studies you should be able to play them memorizing the progression instead every single note.

Canon of Pachelbel

79 Arpeggios with string skipping of the famous progression of **Pachelbel's Canon,** in **sixteenth notes**.

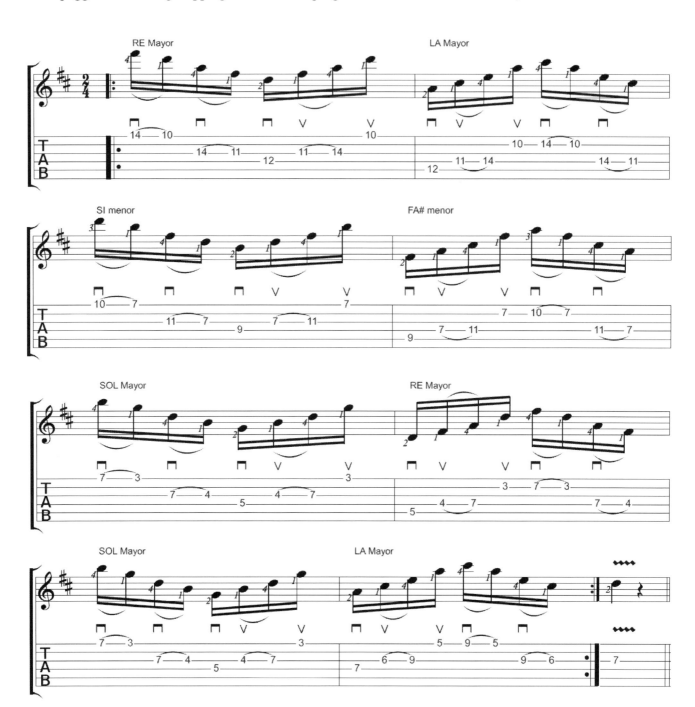

Notice how always is indicated the chord of every arpeggio, it should be the most important thing rather than the notes in the pentagram.

80 Another arrangement with the same progression, now we play in **sextuplet notes**.

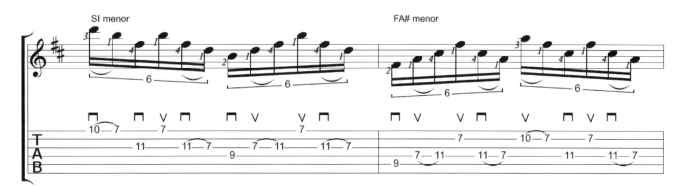

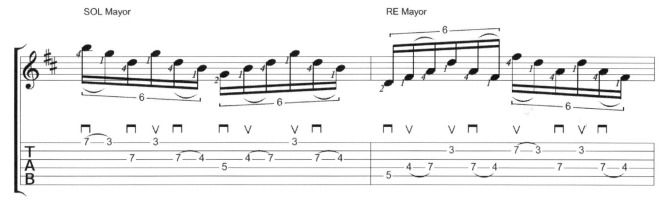

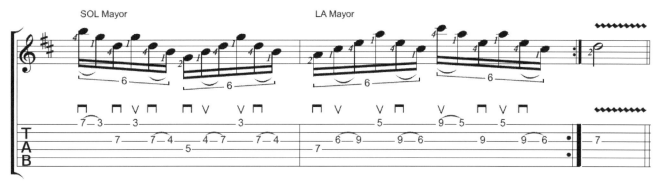

I Will Survive

81 Surely you remember this progression too. It's the song "I will survive" written by Freddie Perren and Dino Fekaris and sung by Gloria Gaynor. Here is an arrangement in sixteenth notes with in a slightly different sequence to what Paul Gilbert frequently uses

82 Same progression, arranged in **sextuplet notes**.

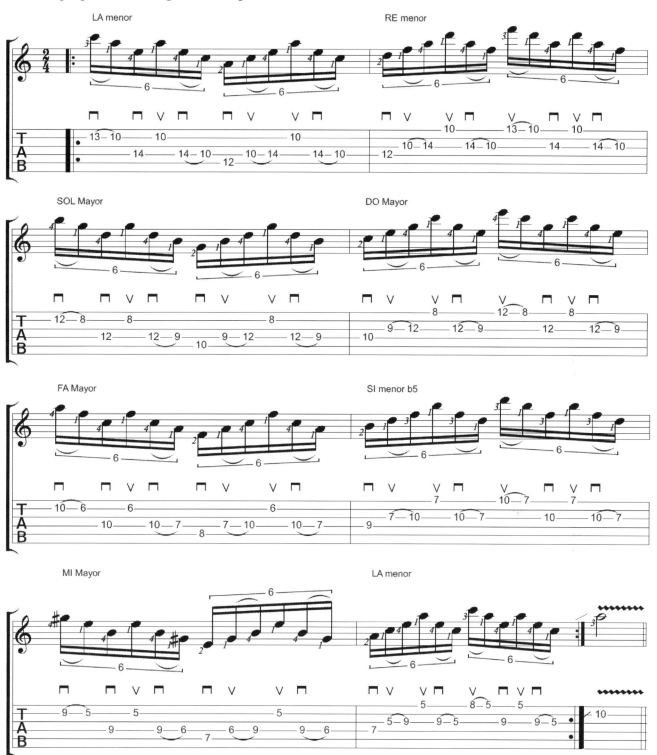

These progressions arranged as a study will help you to develop the technique of **triad arpeggios with string skipping**, and also will inspire you to make your own ideas when using this technique in your own progressions or any that you like.

It would be great, as an exercise, to create your own study.

String skipping with stretching

Paul Gilbert has a big elasticity in his left hand, this allows him to play patterns which require big stretches in the left hand. In the next examples we will see some arpeggios that **Paul Gilbert** plays with string skipping and big stretches.

If you find any trouble at first, you can transport the pattern to the higher frets. Once you feel comfortable come back and try to play them as is written in this book.

Triad arpeggios with string skipping and stretching

83 This is the first example of **string skipping with stretching**, we have an **A minor arpeggio**.

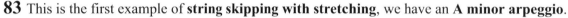
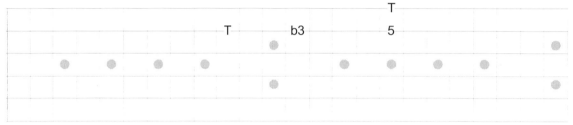

This pattern has nothing to do with the previous **triad arpeggios with string skipping,** in this occasion, instead of a **vertical pattern**, we have a **horizontal** one which requires **left hand stretches to reach the frets proposed**.

Remember to transport the pattern to the higher frets if you are not comfortable. For instance, you could play a **C minor arpeggio** instead of the one proposed.

A minor arpeggio:

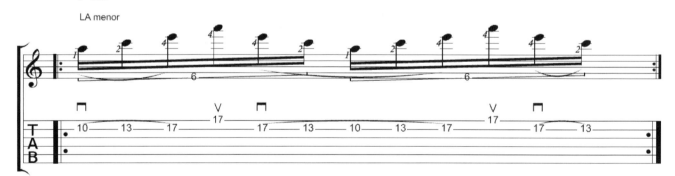

Still there is not a big skip, we are just changing to the string bellow, but it's a good point to start with and to concentrate better in the left hand stretches.

84 In this pattern of **A minor** we have a string skipping, from the 4th string to the 2nd.

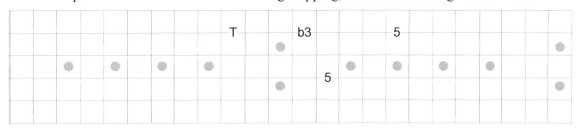

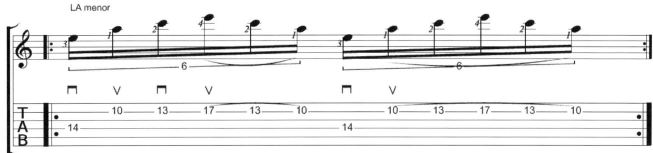

Look at the strokes, there are two different choices. In the first measure the are four pick movements while there are only two in the second. **Paul Gilbert** uses both, practice each possibility separately.

85 This pattern of **A minor** mixes both previous patterns.

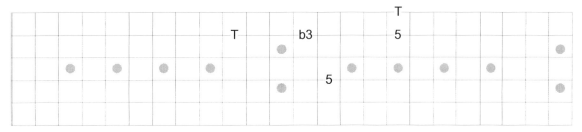

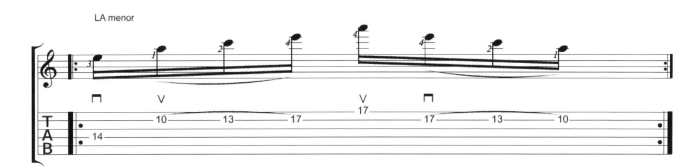

As an exercise you could make and practice **major, diminished and augmented arpeggios** with this last example's idea. You only have to change the third and fifth intervals to achieve the different arpeggios.

Cuatriad arpeggios with string skipping

Paul Gilbert plays very often cuatriad arpeggios with the string skipping technique. In fact, what he almost always plays are **seventh minor arpeggios.**

In the following examples we will see patterns that Gilbert uses for seventh minor arpeggios. **The difficulty will be increasing step by step.**

86 This is a **basic arpeggio pattern** for an **E minor seventh** with string skipping.

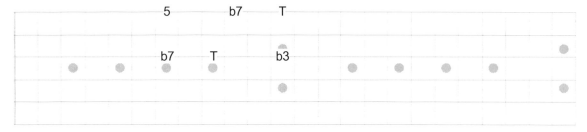

And here it's the proposed exercise. Even though it's in quintuplet notes is very easy to count.

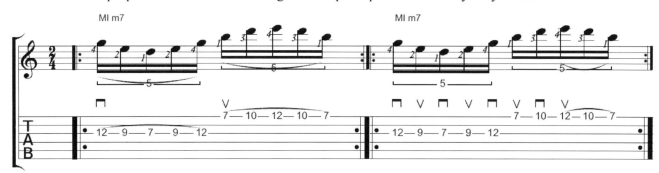

Again there are two different ways of playing the same pattern, make sure you practice both.

87 **E minor seventh** pattern with string skipping from the 5th string to 3th.

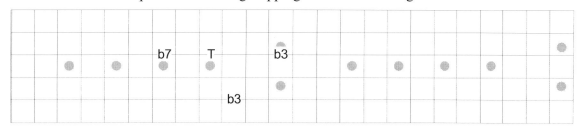

Again two different choices. The first one should be the easiest, practice it as long as you need it and then try the second option.

In this case we are playing sextuplet notes.

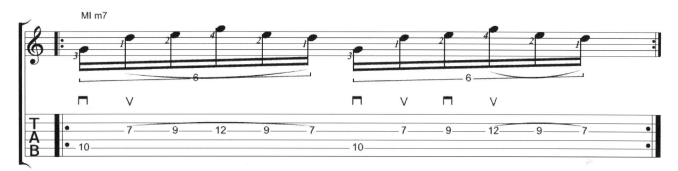

88 **E minor seventh pattern**.

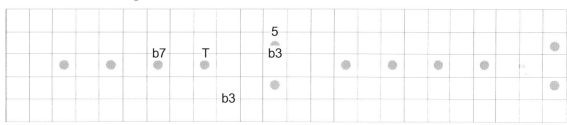

Similar to the previous exercise with a fifth added in the 2nd string. We are playing **sixteenth notes**.

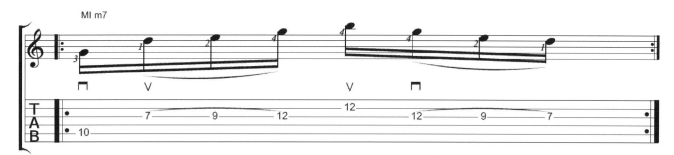

89 E minor seventh pattern with two string skipping.

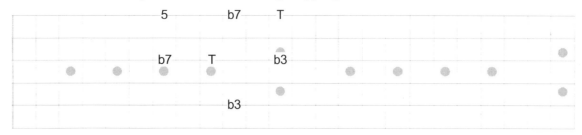

This is the complete **E minor seventh** pattern in sextuplet notes. Maybe this one is more difficult than the previous because of the two string skipping.

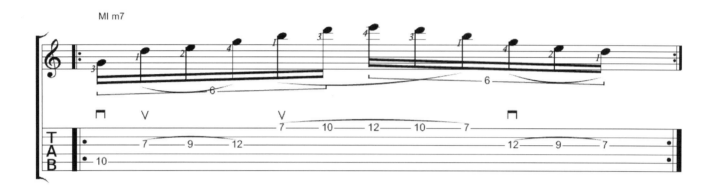

90 Exactly as the exercise above but adding two pick strokes. Adding strokes could complicate its execution.

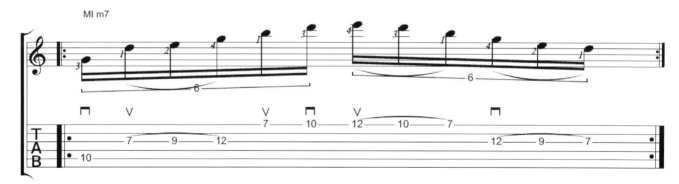

This pick strokes combination is what **Paul Gilbert** uses in this kind of arpeggios with string skipping.

91 **E minor seventh** pattern with **tapping**.

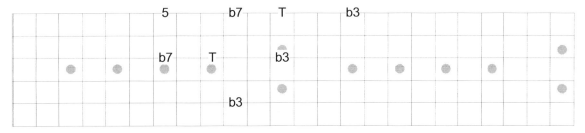

In this example the arpeggio has been extended by adding an extra note (a minor third), we will use the tapping technique. This example is in septuplet notes.

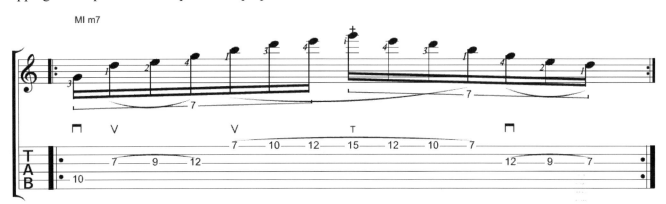

Paul Gilbert uses his index finger to tap, he instantly holds the pick with the middle and thumb fingers, and after tapping comes back to hold his pick with the index and thumb.

This can be tricky, I prefer to tap directly with my middle finger because I don't need to change the way I'm holding my pick. Both forms are correct, use the one is better for you.

92 **E seventh minor** with **tapping** and **slide**.

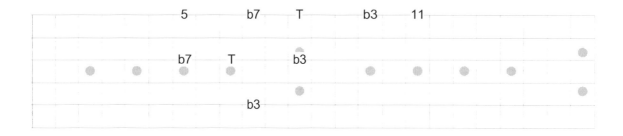

This example is similar to #91, with the tapping idea, but in addition **we extend the arpeggio with a slide, using the same finger, to reach the 4th (or 11th).**

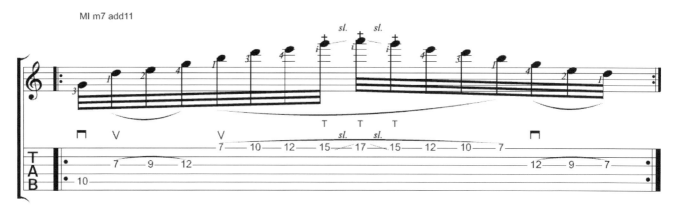

You can modify the length of the slide to the fifth (19 fret), for example. **Paul Gilbert** uses very often this resource, it creates a really fun and interesting effect.

Scales and string skipping

To this point we have seen exclusively **string skipping with arpeggios**, but you can also apply it to **diatonic or pentatonic scales**. The following examples will show how **Paul Gilbert** uses string skipping to scales.

String skipping on scales on a static position

In this example we have string skipping on a static position, this means that there is no displacement through the neck, but only vertically.

93 **C major** scale pattern, 3 notes per string.

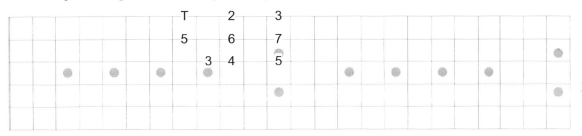

This pattern is what we could call a **static position**, we can only move up and down of the neck.

Pay attention to this first example, practice it as long as you need it before passing to the next more complex examples.

It's in quintuplet notes, but is easy to count because we have five notes in each string. The main problem is the string skipping from the first string to the third and to get every note sounding. **Paul Gilbert** never misses a note, make sure you either.

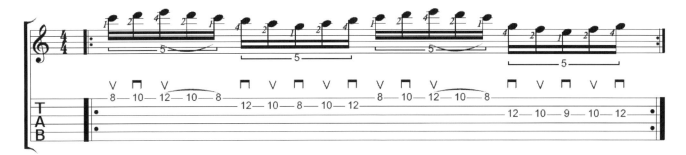

94 **C major** complete pattern, 3 notes per string.

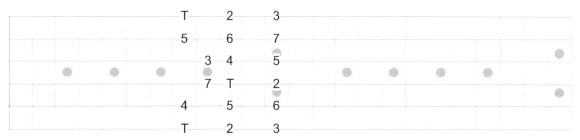

If the previous exercise was difficult, this one is crazy. This is **Paul Gilbert**.

In this example we are changing from the first string to every one of the others. As bigger is the skip, bigger is the difficulty.

Practice it with calm, be patient because this can be really tricky.

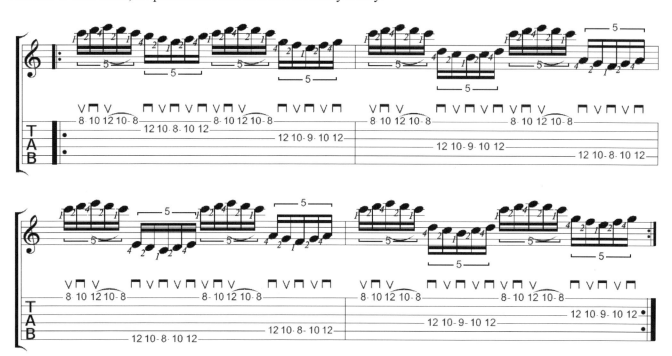

Remember to mute the lower strings, as **Paul Gilbert** would do.

You can modify the exercise if it's too hard. For example, you could concentrate in the three first strings, and once you are comfortable add the next string and so on. You can also practice on concrete strings, like the first and fourth, or first and fifth, etc.

String skipping on scales in horizontal

"Static scales" are those in which we move **vertically**, now we will see **"lineal" scales** in which we will move **horizontally.**

I call **lineal scales** to the scales developed in one or two strings along the neck. In this pattern we can see an example of that. **C major scale.**

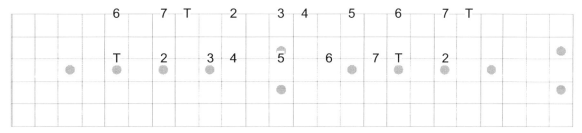

95 Sequence with **string skipping** in **C major** scale.

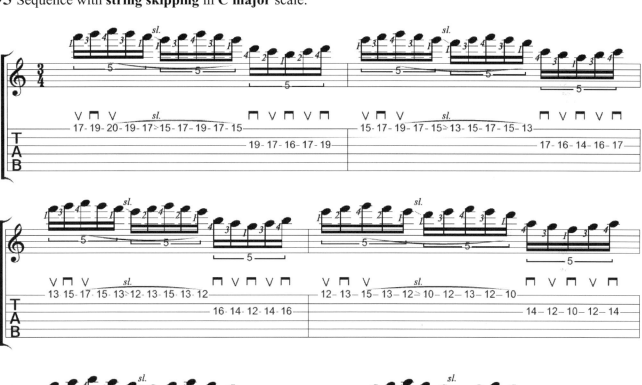

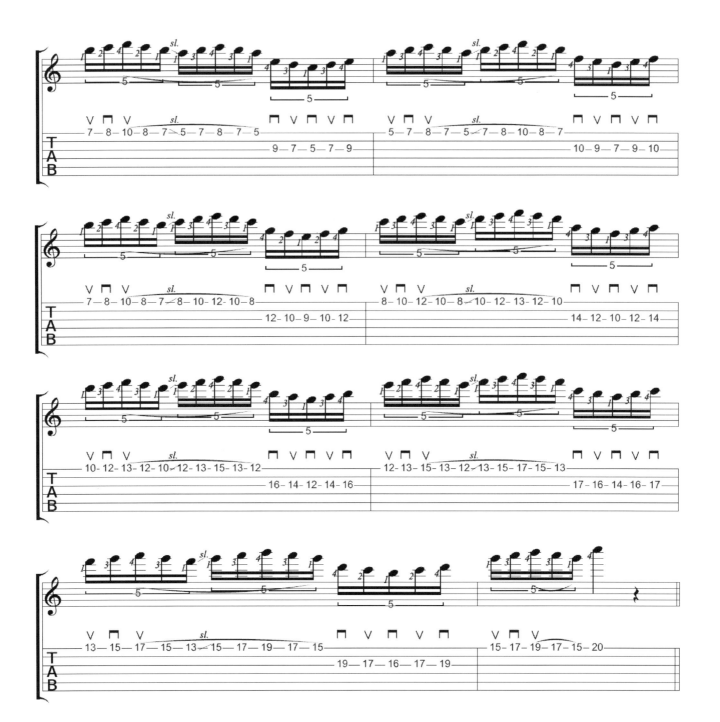

It requires some practice before making it sound properly this kind of phrases, don't give up if you feel it's too difficult at first.

Paul Gilbert likes so much this kind of phrases, he has an unique and spectacular sound when he plays it. As an exercise try the same pattern in other key, as **G major**, **D major**, etc.

Ideas, phrases and exercises
in the style of Paul Gilbert

Paul Gilbert's fingering

In this section we will see a series of ideas, phrases and exercises in the style of **Paul Gilbert**.

The left hand fingering shown in the following examples is not the standard fingering or recommended. In this section, the left hand fingering indicated is the one **Paul Gilbert** would use.

The most noticeable difference between the traditional fingering and the Gilbert one is in finger 3 (ring finger). **Paul Gilbert**, in the patterns of 3 notes per string separated by two tones, uses always the fingers 1 (index), 3 (ring) and 4 (pinky), instead 1, 2 (middle) and 4.

Here is an example, check out the differences commented:

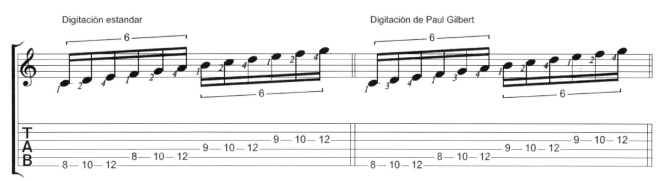

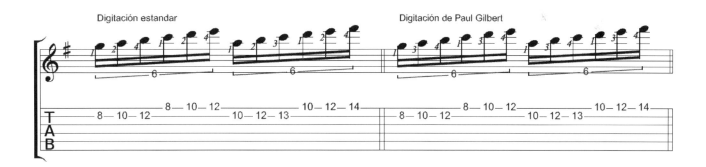

Both fingerings are correct. The important thing is feeling comfortable with any fingering no matter which is. Is for that my comment at the beginning of the book about the fingerings, they are only recommendations, you can change them whenever you want.

But, if you feel comfortable with both fingerings, **¿which one is better?**

The most obvious answer is which you feel more comfortable, to me is better the traditional fingering, what we have seen to this point. I consider it better because to me is more versatile and better to adapt to any style and guitarist. However, if only will be played phrases and licks in the style of **Paul Gilbert** his fingering is pretty efficient (so it looks watching at him).

In principle the fingering of **Paul Gilbert** has some technical advantages because has less fingers changes.

See the next example, with traditional fingering is needed to change the fingering when changing from the 5th to the 4th string, while with the fingering of Paul Gilbert remains the same.

In the anterior example, the fingering of Gilbert may have a slight advantage over the traditional fingering. But this advantage could be reduced if we modify the traditional fingering, instead fingers 1, 2 and 4 for the 6th and 5th strings, we could change it to 1, 2 and 3. With this fingering the second finger (middle) will be instantly ready when passing from the 5th string to the 4th. It may seem a pointless change, but when you are playing fast this little changes can make de difference.

After all, we can conclude that any fingering could be fair, I have shown some options so you can try them and feel which is the best for you. In my case I prefer the "traditional fingering" and in some situations the "modified traditional". Don't worry about modifying fingerings, just try and find your way.

Clarified this issue let's see some examples of sequences, phrases and exercises in the style of **Paul Gilbert**.

Alternate Picking

Ideas, phrases and exercises with the alternate picking technique.

96 Sequence in alternate picking, sextuplet notes.

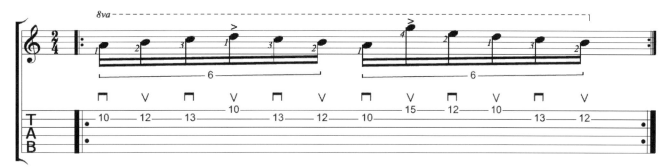

Try to practice it in sixteenth notes too.

97 Sequence of alternate picking on strings 3th and 4th.

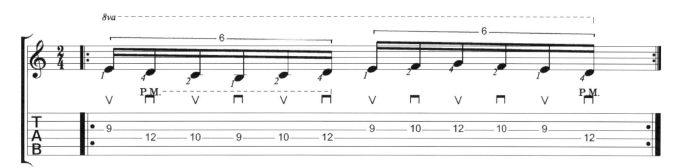

This sequence begins with an upstroke and then a downstroke when changing to the next string ("outside picking"). Remember that Gilbert prefers this kind of sequences. Don't forget to mute the lower strings, you can even play the whole exercise with palm muting

98 Melodic sequence in sixteenth notes.

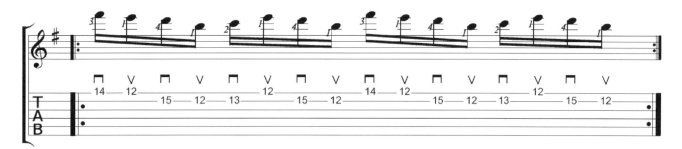

You can apply this sequence over a scale or pattern in two strings, as we have seen in this book.

99 Lineal sequence over one string.

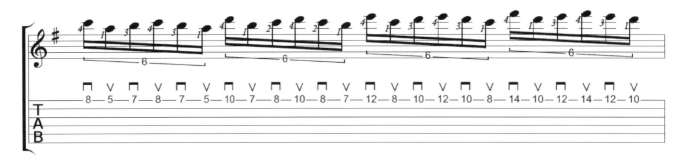

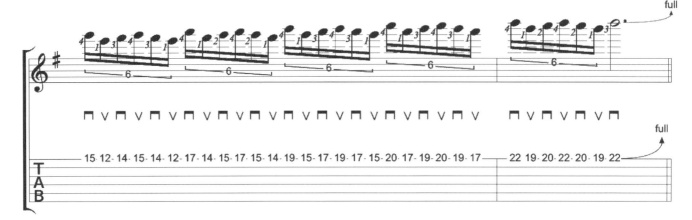

Yngwie Malmsteen uses very often this type of lineal sequences.

100 Sequence with a classic vibe.

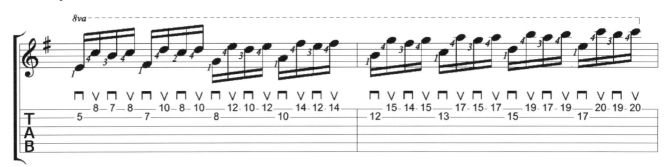

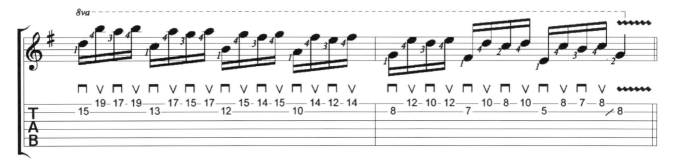

This resource is known as **ostinato**.

101 Melodic sequence, sixteenth notes in **E minor** using a two stringed pattern.

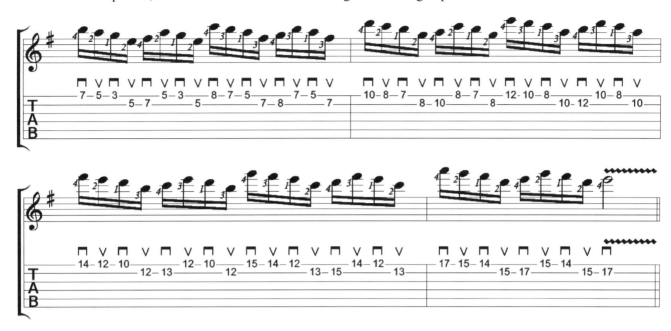

102 This type of sequence is very common in Gilbert, and his sound is so characteristic of him.

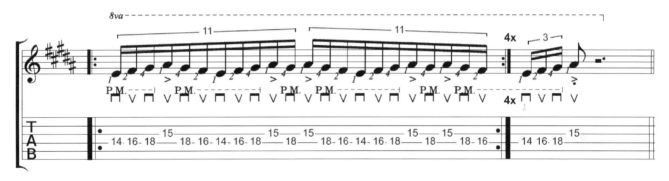

103 Sequence of alternate picking with "inside picking".

You can mute the 4th string, as **Paul Gilbert** would do.

104 Alternate picking with string skipping.

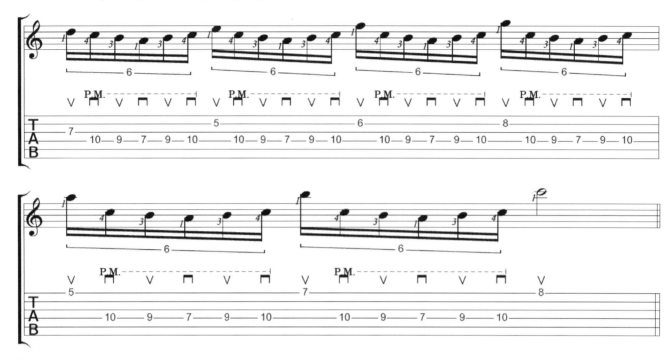

This example uses ostinato too.

105 A harmonic minor scale.

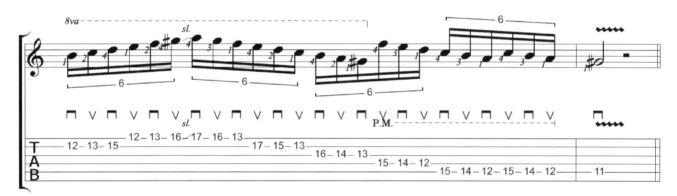

106 Similar example as above but now in **A minor.**

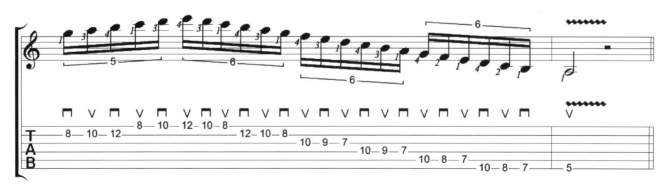

107 Ascending sequence in **C Major**.

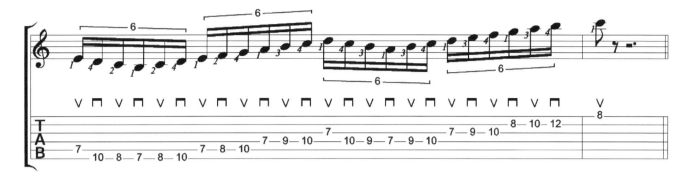

Remember, **Paul Gilbert** mutes the lower strings (6th, 5th and 4th).

108 Descending sequence in **C Major**.

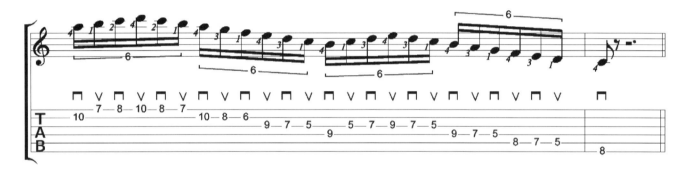

109 Exercise of alternate picking on low strings.

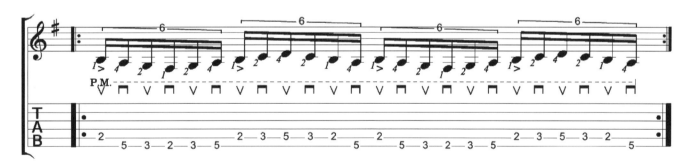

110 Same sequence as the previous exercise, now is developed over **C Major** scale, ascending.

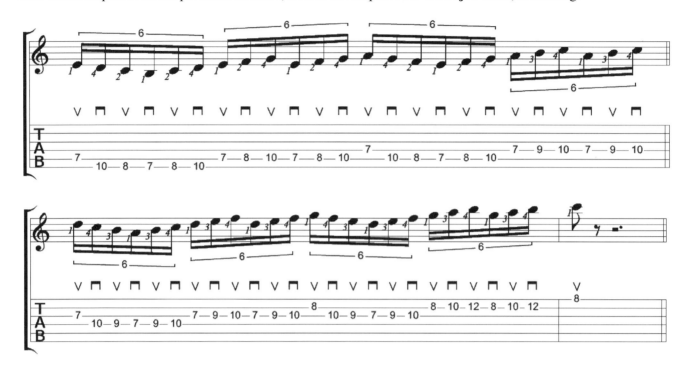

111 Similar to #110, now descending.

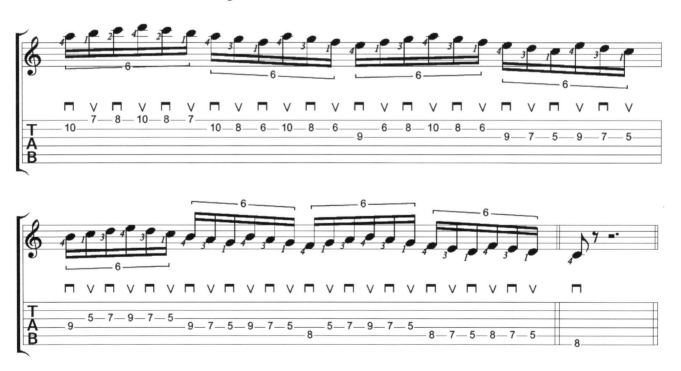

112 This phrase sounds pretty good over a dominant chord.

There are some chromatics in the first bar, which sounds interesting. Even though it has chromatics and notes out of the scale still sounds correct, because in every of the four downbeats there is a note of the **E seventh** arpeggio. In the first beat we have a D (the chord's seventh), second beat is G# (third), third beat is the tonic, and fourth beat is B (fifth).

113 Chromatic scale.

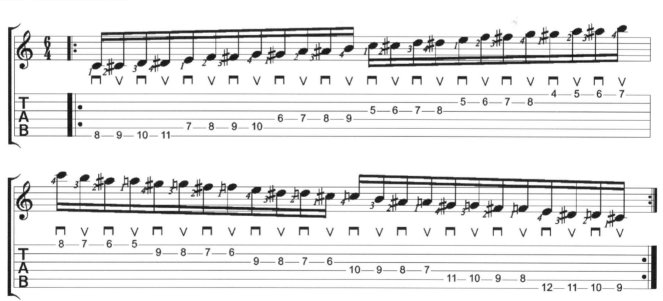

114 Descending sequence in **E Major** scale.

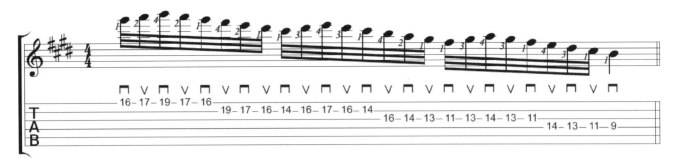

115 Descending sequence in **E Minor** scale, sextuplet notes.

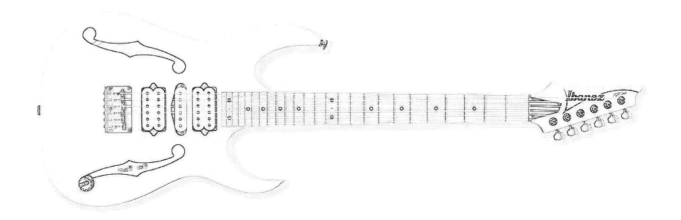

Legato

Ideas, phrases and exercises in which in addition to the alternate picking is used legato too.

116 Lick mixing alternate picking with legato.

117 Legato sequence emphasizing the chromatic of the blue note (Eb).

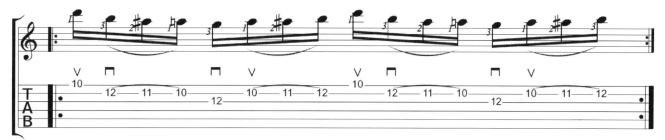

118 This lick combines legato with alternate picking. E minor scale.

119 Sequence with legato and picking over the dorian scale with an added blue note.

120 Exercise combining alternate picking and legato in **A minor**.

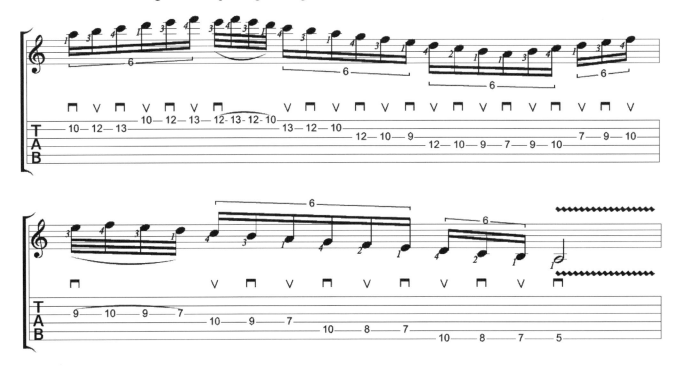

121 Descending phrase in **A harmonic** minor.

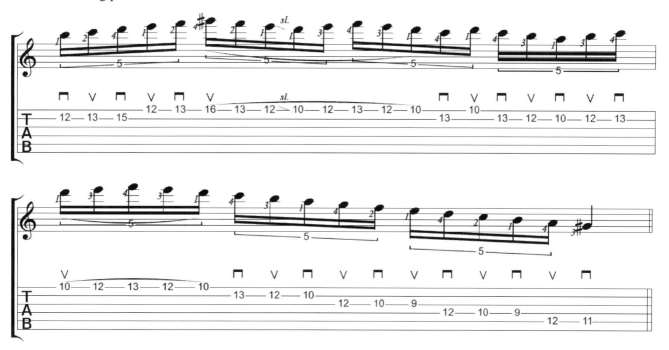

122 Descending sequence in **E minor**.

123 Descending sequence in **A harmonic minor**.

124 Descending phrase in **E minor pentatonic** using a 3 notes per string pattern.

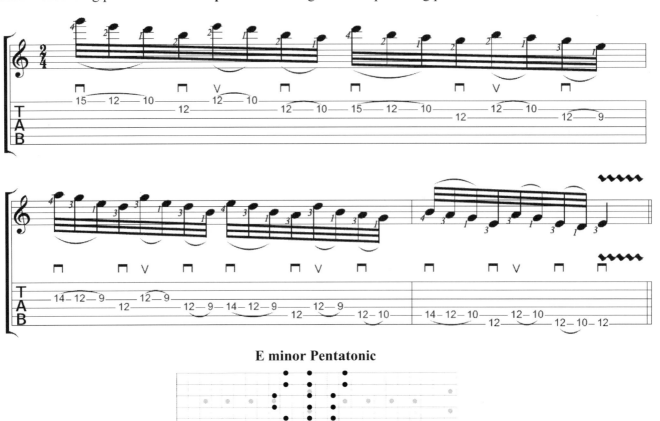

E minor Pentatonic

125 Descending phrase in **A minor pentatonic** with an added **blue note**.

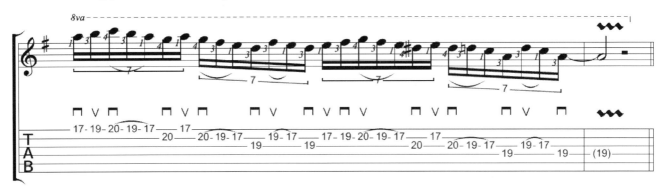

126 Exactly the same exercise but an octave lower.

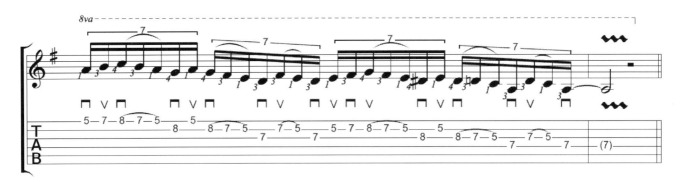

127 Sequence on one string in **E minor** combining alternate picking with legato.

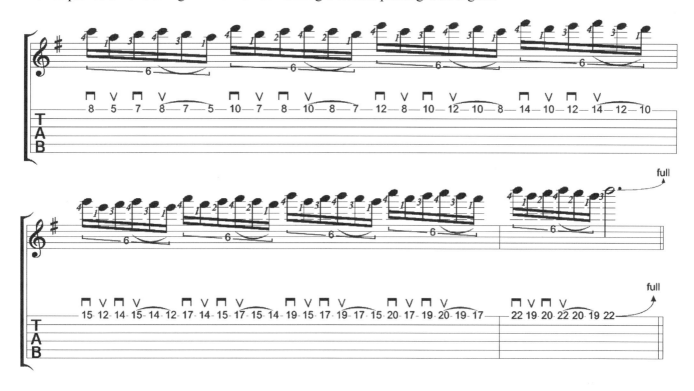

128 **C major** arpeggio with some added tensions.

129 Add 9 arpeggio of **G# Major**.

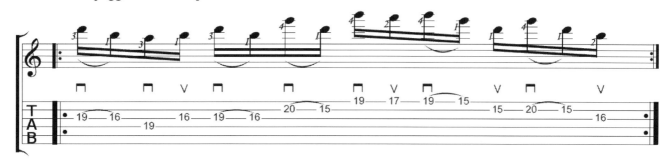

130 Ascending sequence in **G Major**, **sextuplet notes**.

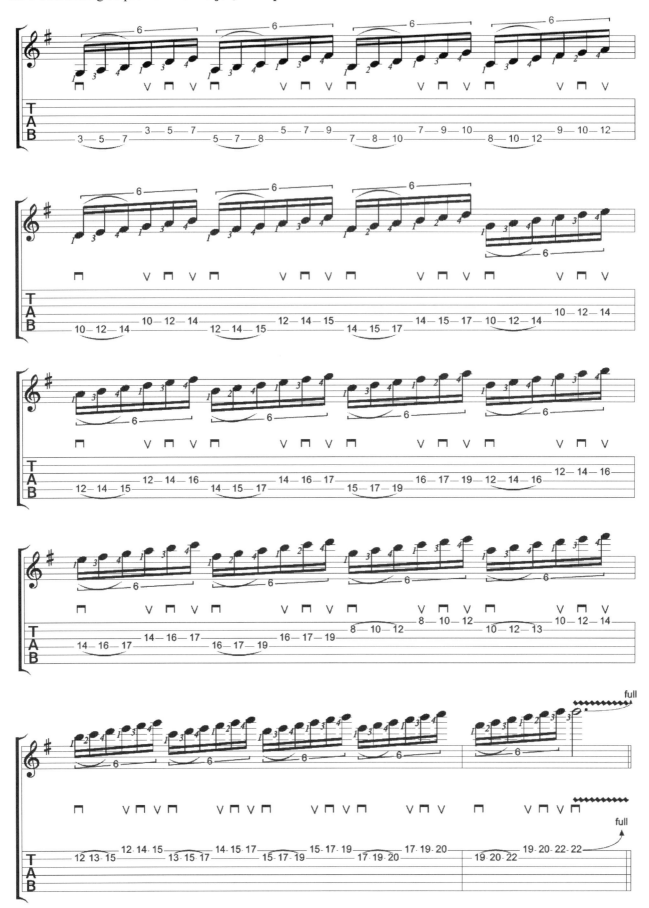

131 Descending sequence in **G Major**, **sextuplet notes**.

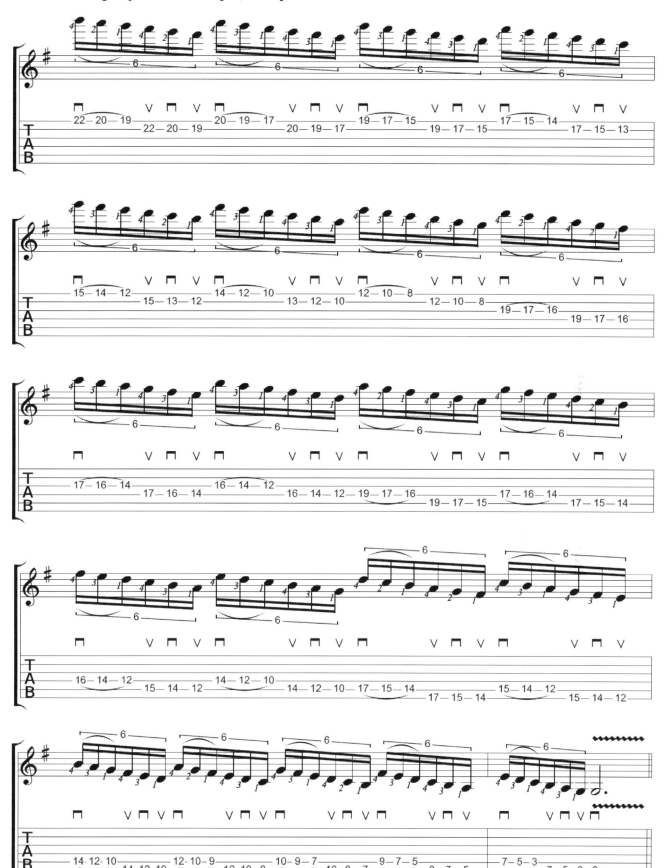

132 Ascending sequence in **E minor pentatonic**, **sextuplet notes**.

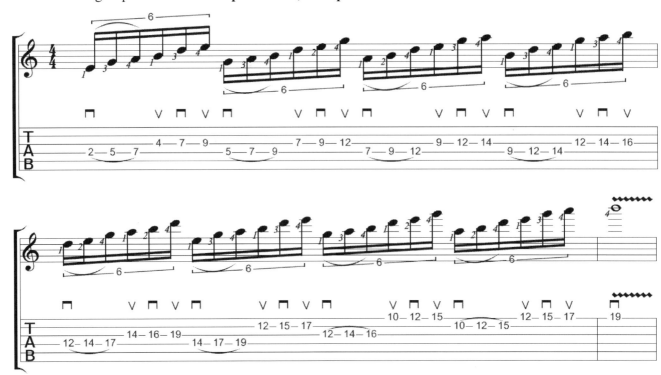

133 Descending sequence in **E minor pentatonic**, **sextuplet notes**.

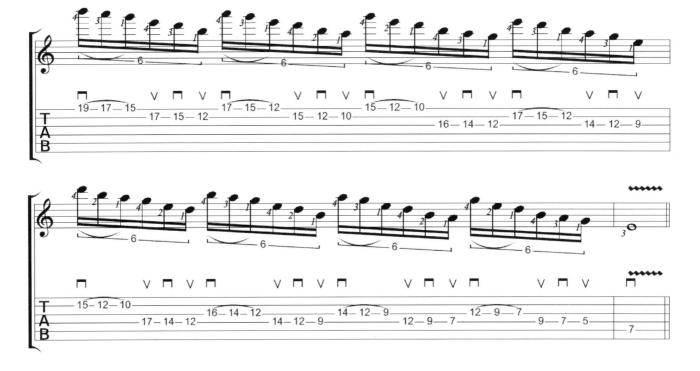

String skipping

134 **C Major add11** arpeggio with string skipping.

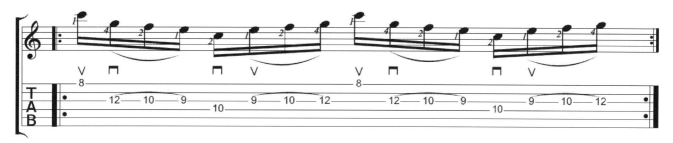

135 **C Major add9 add11** arpeggio with string skipping.

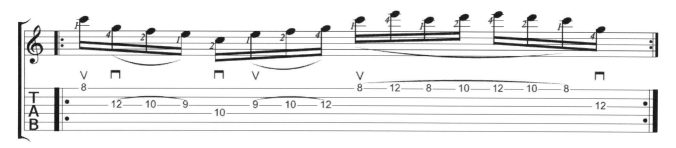

136 **F# minor seventh** with string skipping and stretching.

137 **A minor seventh** arpeggio with string skipping.

138 **E diminished seventh** with string skipping and stretching.

139 **G# diminished seventh** with string skipping and stretching

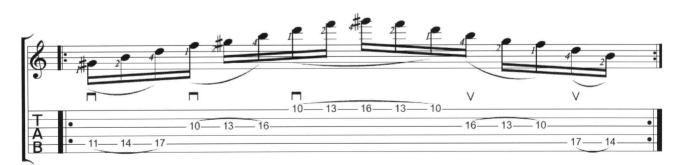

140 B diminished seventh with string skipping and stretching.

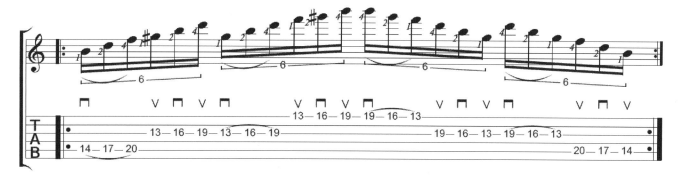

This arpeggio is a bit easier than the arpeggio in exercise 139, fret distance is smaller. When you feel is too hard to do any exercise like this move it to higher frets as much as is necessary, once you have nailed it move back to lower frets. In contrast, if it's too easy move it to lower frets.

141 Static sequence with alternate picking and string skipping.

This example begins with an upstroke in order of maintaining the "outside picking". Is very difficult to play string skipping with inside picking.

142 Exercise in **A minor** with alternate picking and string skipping.

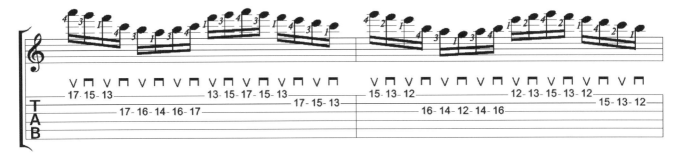

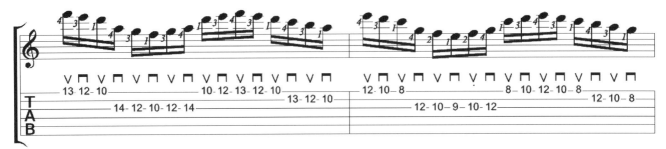

143 Exercise in **E harmonic minor** with string skipping.

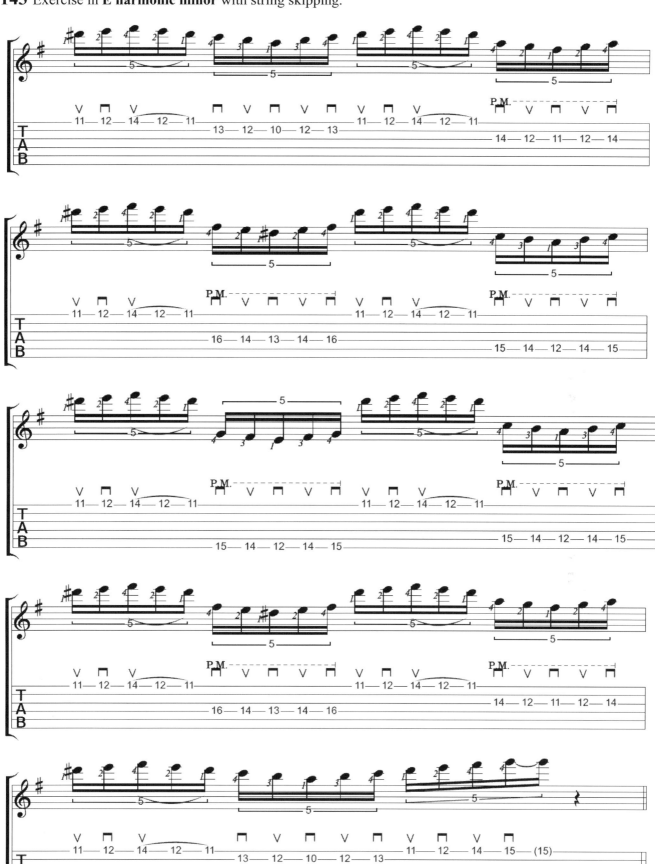

Tapping

Ideas, phrases and exercises with tapping. **Paul Gilbert** does not stand out by his tapping technique, however he frequently uses a very interesting ideas. In this section we will see some of them.

144 **Ascending A minor arpeggio** with tapping.

145 **Descending A minor arpeggio** with tapping.

146 **Ascending A minor arpeggio** with tapping in sextuplet notes.

147 Descending A minor arpeggio with tapping in sextuplet notes.

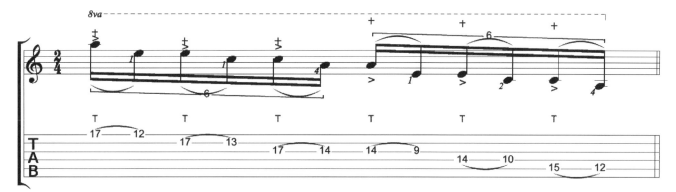

148 A minor seventh arpeggio with **string skipping** and **tapping**.

Sweep Picking

Paul Gilbert has a very clean sweep picking technique, but he rarely uses it. Usually he would do an ascending sweep, from the lower strings to the higher at the beginning of some of his phrases.

Anyway, even though he prefers other techniques to play arpeggios, as the string skipping, he uses sweep picking on occasion. In this section we will see some of the patterns of arpeggios with sweep picking that are the most used by **Paul Gilbert.**

149 **E minor** arpeggio with sweep picking (6 strings).

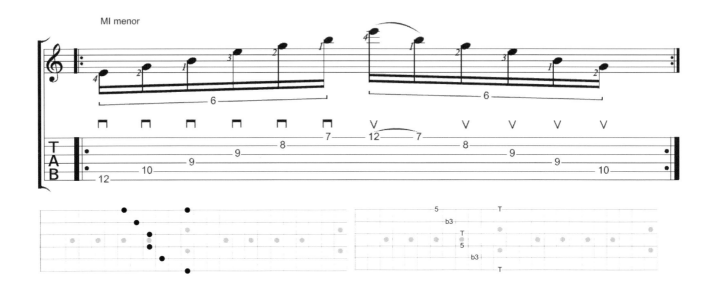

150 **F Major** arpeggio with sweep picking (6 strings).

151 Arpeggio of **A minor** with sweep picking (5 strings).

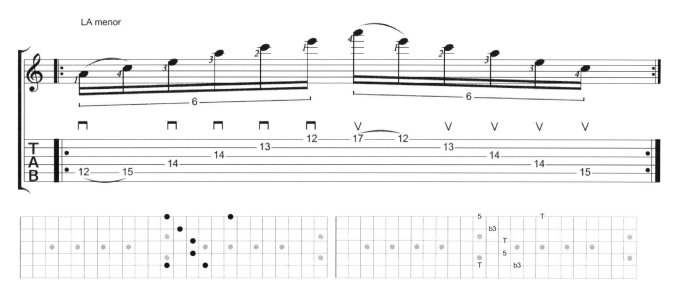

152 Arpeggio of **G Major** with sweep picking (5 strings).

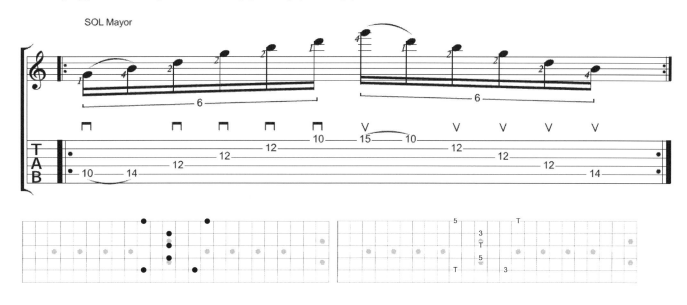

153 Arpeggio of **A minor** with sweep picking (5 strings), this is a different pattern from example 151.

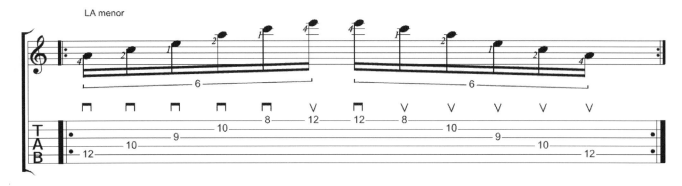

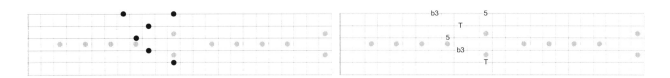

154 Arpeggio of **C Major** with sweep picking (5 strings).

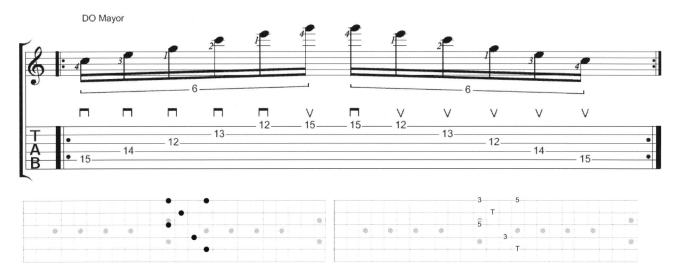

108

Conclusion:

If you got here surely is because you have already practiced every exercise in the book, unless you are like me, starting books from the last pages … anyway, the important thing is that you are reading the final page of this book which I appreciate.

In the case you have practiced every exercise is more than presumable that, in addition of have learned some new things, your technique will have improved. However, this is not the end, just the beginning. Now you could practice again all the exercises taking note of at what speed you are able to play and sound properly for every exercise. Yes, this book can be heavy … but books are made to use them, not for leaving them in a shelf. It doesn't matter how fast or slow you play the exercises, just play them again and take note of your speed **once you have reached a good tone and technique.**

Surely you listened several times that speed does not matter and it will arrive with time, but this is not exactly true, speed won't arrive if you don't look for it. And speed is not the main goal, of course, but it's truly important in the style of **Paul Gilbert**. ¿Could you imagine of **Paul Gilbert** without his fast phrases? ¿Do you think he could have become that great guitarist if he wouldn't had his control of speed? That is ...

Well, let's suppose you practiced again every exercise, using metronome and taking notes of the speed. In this point you could leave this book for a while, study other things and in a couple of months return to it to practice them again. If everything went alright is more than possible that with only a bit of practice you could play them better and faster. This is a good way of using this book, every now and then returning to it and see how much you are improving.

Personally I like to include many aspects in my practice time, this manner of study works for me but there are others. For instance, if you are really interested in the style of **Paul Gilbert**, instead of using this book from time to time you could add it in your practice time for an undefined period.

Any option is fine, the most important is to not stop of learning and practicing. Whatever is the way you use this book I'm confident that practicing this exercises proposed it will improve your technique

Good luck, and above all **have fun** playing in style of **Paul Gilbert**!

Thanks a thousand Paul!

Toni Lloret

Printed in Poland
by Amazon Fulfillment
Poland Sp. z o.o., Wrocław